CALIFORNIA NATURAL HISTORY GUIDES

INTRODUCTION TO
CALIFORNIA'S BEACHES AND COAST

California Natural History Guides

Phyllis M. Faber and Bruce M. Pavlik, General Editors

Introduction to
CALIFORNIA'S BEACHES AND COAST

Gary Griggs

UNIVERSITY OF CALIFORNIA PRESS

Berkeley   Los Angeles   London

California Natural History Guides No. 99

University of California Press, one of the most distinguished university presses in the United States, enriches lives around the world by advancing scholarship in the humanities, social sciences, and natural sciences. Its activities are supported by the UC Press Foundation and by philanthropic contributions from individuals and institutions. For more information, visit www.ucpress.edu.

University of California Press
Berkeley and Los Angeles, California

University of California Press, Ltd.
London, England

© 2010 by the Regents of the University of California

Library of Congress Cataloging-in-Publication Data

Griggs, Gary B.
    Introduction to California's beaches and coast / Gary Griggs.
        p. cm. – (California natural history guides ; no. 99)
    Includes index.
    ISBN 978-0-520-26289-8 (cloth : alk. paper) — ISBN 978-0-520-26290-4 (pbk. : alk. paper)
    1. Coasts—California. 2. Coast changes—California. 3. Natural history—California—Pacific Coast. I. Title.

GB458.8.G75 2010

551.45'709794--dc22   2009050657

Manufactured in China

16   15   14   13   12   11   10

10   9   8   7   6   5   4   3   2   1

The paper used in this publication meets the minimum requirements of ANSI/NISO Z39.48-1992 (R 1997) (*Permanence of Paper*).∞

Cover illustration: Kenneth and Gabrielle Adelman, Coastal Records Project, www.californiacoastline.org.

The publisher gratefully acknowledges the generous
contributions to this book provided by

the Gordon and Betty Moore Fund
in Environmental Sciences

and

the General Endowment Fund of the
University of California Press Foundation

CONTENTS

INTRODUCTION

A PERSONAL PERSPECTIVE ON THE COAST AND BEACHES OF CALIFORNIA

California's 1,100-mile coastline has something to offer almost everybody, whether resident or visitor, young or old, athletic or sedentary. There are sunny southern California beaches where you can join thousands of others to escape the heat of the city on a summer day (Figure 1) or, at the other extreme, some wild and isolated stretch of shoreline where you can still find solitude and peace of mind while exploring for shells, pebbles, and driftwood (Figure 2). California has one of the most spectacular and diverse coastlines in the country: high mountains plummeting to sheer rocky cliffs, long stretches of sandy beach, and extensive marshes and wetlands. It is a state that in many ways is defined by its coast, and it is then little wonder that such an environment draws people to the shore. Yet, the shoreline is also the battleground between land and sea, a line that is constantly migrating as sea level rises and falls in response to global climate change.

The magnetic attraction of California's shoreline is summarized in a single statistic: 80 percent of the state's 38 million people live within an hour of the coast, and this number continues to increase. California's coastal counties have 24% of the state's area but 75% of the population and 80% of the jobs. If we divided up the coastline evenly among its residents, these 38 million people would each have a little less than two inches of oceanfront, hardly enough to enjoy. It's not quite that grim, however. If we look at California's actual area of beach sand, we each have about 24 square feet, just

Figure 1. A crowded day at Main Beach in Santa Cruz. Photo Gary Griggs.

enough for a large beach towel. The state's residents must also share the beaches with about 32 million visitors each year, which further reduces their space. We don't usually all go to the beach at the same time, although it often seems that way in parts of southern California. North of Santa Barbara, however, with the possible exception of the Boardwalk or Main Beach in Santa Cruz, it's not too difficult to find a quiet beach to explore and enjoy.

California's coastline and beaches are amazingly diverse—it is one of the first things that visitors from Florida, Texas or New Jersey notice on a trip along our coastline. It doesn't look like Coney Island, Galveston, or Miami Beach. Lots of diverse forces and processes interact on the coast, making the coastline one of the world's most dynamic environments. Waves, tides, wind, storms, rain, and runoff combine to build up, wear down, and continually reshape the interface of land and sea. Many California coastal cliffs are eroding relatively quickly (a foot or so a year) and

Figure 2. Getting to the beach at the mouth of the Big Sur River in Molera State Park requires a hike, but you are rewarded with a beautiful, uncrowded coastline and purple sand. Photo Kenneth and Gabrielle Adelman, California Coastal Records Project, www .CaliforniaCoastline.org.

beaches can disappear overnight. These recurring events gain front-page headlines when some celebrity's home is threatened—"MOVIE STARS' OCEAN FRONT HOMES BATTERED BY WAVES IN MALIBU." In reality, the entire 1,100 miles of the state's shoreline are slowly retreating, regardless of whether the property is owned by movie stars or dot-com executives.

While walking along the shoreline, whether at Solana Beach, Malibu, Santa Barbara, Stinson Beach, or countless other places along California's coast, you are likely to see sandy beaches backed by dunes, low bluffs, or abrupt cliffs on one side and the repeated run-up of waves onto the shore on the other. Perhaps this scene evokes a sense of beauty and energy and a feeling of permanence or even timelessness. Such a feeling, however, can be misleading. Each feature of the coast—whether steep cliffs, sand dunes, or the beach itself—is dynamic and delicately balanced with the processes that shape the shoreline, such as the action of waves,

Figure 3. Wide, sandy southern California beach at Hermosa Beach. Photo Kenneth and Gabrielle Adelman, California Coastal Records Project, www.CaliforniaCoastline.org.

tides, and winds; these all change from day to day, month to month, and year to year.

Millions of people and billions of dollars in structures and development now lie within a few feet of a sea level that is constantly changing (Figure 3). For a part of our state that we identify with so closely, that so many of us are drawn to so strongly, and that in some ways is our edge and our stability, it can be a bit unsettling that this coastline isn't stable and that its not in the same place today that it was a decade ago. Yet this is what makes it exciting and interesting. Each year or each storm brings a different set of conditions, so that the coastline rarely looks the same for very long. Winter storms take away the sand and perhaps some of the bluff, but they also uncover new treasures and leave driftwood and other things behind. The next summer will return a slightly different beach, perhaps wider or maybe narrower. For the infrequent visitor these changes are unexpected, but to a resident, they are certain and keep bringing us back.

For an oceanfront property owner, however, large storm waves, particularly when arriving simultaneously with a high tide, can be a nightmare. Herein lies a serious dilemma; much of California's and the world's population has built right up to the edge in many cases, even though the shoreline is constantly changing and migrating. The dimensions of the state's oceanfront parcels have been surveyed and recorded down to a hundredth of a foot, but the Pacific Ocean is 10,000 miles wide, and it doesn't care much about a few feet either way at the margins. Not surprisingly, there are many California oceanfront parcels that were created 50 or 100 years ago that are now completely beneath the waves.

If we could look back in time about 18,000 years, we would find that the climate was considerably cooler than today and that Earth was in the waning stages of a period of extensive glaciation. Nearly 11 million cubic miles of seawater was bound up on the continents in the form of ice caps and glaciers that covered a significant portion of Earth's surface, including large parts of North America and Europe. The removal of this seawater from the oceans led to a worldwide drop in sea level of about 350 to 400 feet. As a result, the shoreline along the coast of California at that time was about five to 25 miles offshore to the west of its present location (Figure 4). You could have taken a day's hike out to the Farallon Islands off of San Francisco, jogged over to Alcatraz, and you wouldn't have needed the Bay Bridge to get from San Francisco to Berkeley. As the climate gradually warmed, the ice caps began to melt and the glaciers slowly retreated. The resulting melt water flowed into the ocean and sea level rose globally at an average rate of nearly half an inch a year, flooding all that offshore real estate. From about 5,000 years ago to the present, the rate of global sea level rise slowed; although, it has continued at about a tenth of an inch annually for the past century. As the ocean basins have gradually filled, the shoreline has moved progressively inland. This has happened repeatedly throughout the glacial and interglacial,

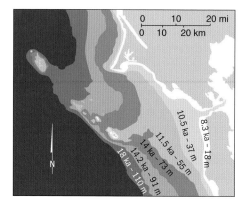

Figure 4. A bathymetric map of the seafloor off San Francisco indicates where the shoreline was at different times over the past 18,000 years. Water depths are in meters (m) and time is given in thousands of years (18ka = 18,000 years ago).

or cool and warm, periods of the past several million years. The advance and retreat of the shoreline wasn't of any significance for over 99% of the period of human occupation of California, but today it is of major concern and adapting to sea level rise has become a big challenge for state and local governments. How would you deal with a three-foot rise in sea level over the next century?

If it is of any consolation, California is not the only state with coastline retreat problems. The shoreline of almost every coastal state is retreating and the low, sandy shorelines, common along the South Atlantic and Gulf coasts, typically erode more rapidly than California's more resistant and usually higher relief coastline. Atlantic and Gulf coast residents also live under the constant threat of hurricanes, whereas we have only earthquakes, El Niños, and an occasional tsunami.

What are the weather patterns that affect the coast of California and what drives the waves that are constantly shaping and reshaping our shoreline? The presence of loose sand and driftwood high on the berm or the back-beach indicates that this stretch of shoreline has been regularly washed over by waves and high tides. Although a particular beach may appear high, wide, and stable during the summer months, it can disappear almost overnight during a severe winter storm. Where does the sand go in the winter months when it's not on the beach and where does our beach sand come from to begin with? Why do some California beaches have black sand, others green sand, and still others pink?

These are but a few of many questions that often perplex the California resident and visitor alike. Accordingly, this book is an exploration of the coast and beaches of California, from the perspective of someone who has spent 45 years studying it, with the goal of trying to help all readers to better understand and appreciate this exceptional shoreline and why it looks and works like it does. Let's take a closer look.

Thinking Geologically

California's coast reflects a complex geological history and the interplay of tectonic or mountain-building processes, geology, climate, and the sea. Huntington Beach, Malibu, Santa Cruz, and Mendocino all look very different as a result of their geological histories, and each has a story to tell if we can sort out all the evidence and assemble the pieces. This is the job of a geologist: to look at the landforms, to study the rocks exposed along the coastline, to observe the processes taking place today, and then to put this in the framework of the whole state (the entire globe, for that matter) in an attempt to understand why each part of the landscape looks the way it does—and, finally, to make an educated guess at how what we see today has evolved. Geologists are really detectives, looking for clues and uncovering evidence that will allow them to draw the most logical conclusions possible as they try to sort out the meaning of a rock outcrop or analyze the sand or pebbles on a beach. Whether a nearly horizontal, uplifted marine terrace in Encinitas, a broad sandy beach in Santa Monica, or a steep coastal cliff in Humboldt County, each region of the coast has a different history. This history—the evolution of and changes along different sections of the state's coast—provides a perspective on the scale of geological change that has taken place and what we might expect in the future, and also allows us to appreciate how fortunate we are to live here. Somehow, knowing that the granite of the Monterey Peninsula or at Bodega Head was formerly a part of the Sierra Nevada, and has been transported 200 miles north along the San Andreas Fault over the past 20 million years, makes our next trip to the coast even more interesting and exciting, and also leads to more questions.

Assembling the Pieces:
The Geologic Origin of California

Early explorers in California quickly became aware of the diverse landscape and topography of the state and the difficulties of traversing the Sierra Nevada and the Coast Ranges, particularly after the relatively easy travel across the monotonous plains and prairies of the mid-continent. Interstate highways have eliminated the adventure and most of the danger, but the state's formidable topography is still hard to avoid. It was not until the great San Francisco earthquake of 1906 that the California residents first became aware of the state's dynamic nature. A large fragment of coastal California, hundreds of miles long, slid northwest as much as 15 feet along the San Andreas Fault (Figure 5). This all came as surprise to nearly everyone living in California

Figure 5. During the 1906 San Francisco earthquake a maximum surface offset of about 15 feet was recorded near Olema, north of San Francisco. Photo G.K. Gilbert, United States Geological Survey.

at the time. It also led to the nearly complete loss of San Francisco and heavy damage to many other cities. A few years later, in 1915, Mt. Lassen, one of the southernmost of the chain of Cascade volcanoes that stretches through northern California, Oregon, Washington and into British Columbia, erupted and offered another glimpse of the area's unstable geological foundation. Subsequent major earthquakes in Santa Barbara in 1927, Long Beach in 1933, Bakersfield in 1952, San Fernando Valley in 1971 and 1994, and the Santa Cruz Mountains in 1989 (Figure 6), have provided decadal reminders that California is in its geological adolescence and does not remain silent for long. None of these events, however, have deterred more people from moving to California; rather, they contributed to the mystique and craziness that often seems to characterize the state. There is a perception, at least in the minds of some, that the people of a region tend to reflect its geologic setting, and few would

Figure 6. The 1989 Loma Prieta earthquake generated large landslides on the steep cliffs of Daly City as far as 60 miles from the epicenter. Photo Gary Griggs.

Figure 7. The steep, rugged topography of the Marin Headlands. Photo Kenneth and Gabrielle Adelman, California Coastal Records Project, www.CaliforniaCoastline.org.

probably argue that Kansas and California are unique in both regards.

The recent geological history of the coast of California, as well as Oregon and Washington, is strikingly different from that of the South Atlantic and Gulf coasts of the United States. Even a casual visitor to the coastline notices the differences between the coastal mountains and sea cliffs that characterize much of California's coast (Figure 7) and the broad, flat coastal plain, sand dunes, and barrier islands of South Carolina or Virginia (Figure 8). California is a state of superlatives; it is the eighth largest economy in the world, the most populous state, and has the highest and lowest points in the lower 48 states (14,805 feet at Mount Whitney and –282 feet in Death Valley). The highest point in Florida is only 345 feet above sea level. Florida is old geologically and is not moving around much these days. Other than an occasional hurricane, and a rising sea level and retreating shoreline, it is a great place to retire. While many come to California to

Figure 8. Fire Island is one of many barrier islands along the east coast of the United States. Photo Cheryl Hapke, United States Geological Survey.

retire, the state is young and active, with regular outbursts of unpredictable activity of all sorts, geological and otherwise.

The 1960s and 1970s witnessed a revolution in scientific thinking about Earth and its history and evolution. Much of the initial evidence for the developing theories and concepts came from the exploration of the ocean basins, which began in earnest in the 1950s. The discovery of a world-encircling undersea ocean ridge that was volcanically active, a system of deep ocean trenches surrounding the Pacific Ocean with associated chains of active volcanoes (the "Ring of Fire"), and a worldwide band of earthquakes that followed these unique features, led to the development of the theory of global or plate tectonics in 1968. New, exciting, and somewhat controversial 40 years ago, this theory now forms part of the basic geological history of Earth that our children and grandchildren learn about in elementary school. Plate tectonics provides a comprehensive framework and explanation for the origin of the large-scale features of Earth—the mountain ranges, volcanoes, trenches, earthquakes and faults—and how they all fit together. California is like a huge Imax theatre of geologic change, if you cannot see some interesting geology outside your kitchen window, you can usually drive a few miles in any direction and you soon will. It's different for Midwesterners, most of them need to drive half way across the state to see some geologic history or find a rock worth writing home about.

Because of the heat within Earth, the interior of the planet is partially molten in places, and therefore weak and somewhat mobile. This hot fluid material slowly rises, owing to its lower density, much like a pot of water heated on the stove. Where the fluid material reaches the surface, along the ocean floor for the most part, the seafloor cracks open and new ocean crust is created. This process has created a globe encircling volcanic mountain range thousands of miles long that passes through all the world's ocean basins: the mid-Atlantic Ridge, the mid-Indian Ridge and the East Pacific Ridge. The hot material beneath the surface spreads out in both directions (a process known as sea floor spreading), carrying along Earth's crust, the ocean floor, and the overlying continents as it moves (Figure 9).

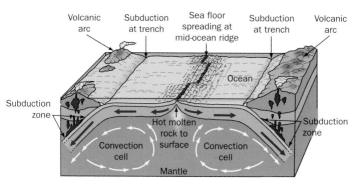

Figure 9. Cross section of Earth's interior illustrating convection cells within the mantle that drive plate motion.

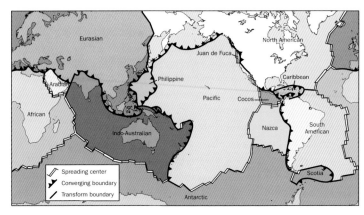

Figure 10. The Earth's major plates, showing motion and types of boundaries between individual plates.

We now recognize that Earth's surface consists of eight to 12 large, thin (about 60 miles thick), rigid plates that move around relative to each other at different speeds, driven in part by the flow of hot fluid material beneath them (Figure 10). Much like large icebergs floating in the ocean, these plates are in constant, although slow, motion (one to several inches per year). At their edges these plates may diverge, collide, or grind past one another. The interaction at the edges of these huge plates leads to tectonically active regions where most of the world's earthquakes occur. In fact, it was the recognition of the concentrated global distribution of these zones of earthquakes that led seismologists to first recognize and sketch out the boundaries of the plates (Figure 11).

The coastal region of California is the place where one very large tectonic plate (the North American Plate) collided with the much smaller Farallon Plate (to the west) for nearly 100 million years (Figure 12). This collision and the resulting plate interactions produced much of the unique and dynamic landscape along California's coast. Most of

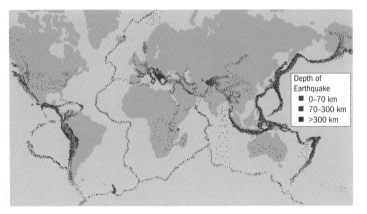

Figure 11. The distribution of global seismicity or earthquakes outlines plate boundaries.

what you see exposed today as you drive along State Hwy, 1, the severely distorted rocks of Devil's Slide and the Marin Headlands, the uplifted terraces of Pacific Palisades, and the rugged mountains rising nearly vertically from the sea along the Big Sur coast, owe their existence to millions of years of tectonic upheaval. As the two plates met, the thinner and denser Farallon oceanic plate to the west was carried down beneath the thicker and lighter continental plate to the east, creating a deep depression or offshore trench that gradually filled with sediments eroded from the mountains of ancestral California. Where the oceanic plate was forced downward under the advancing North American continent, a plunging zone of earthquakes (a subduction zone) formed.

The friction between the plates also scraped off massive volumes of seafloor sediment as well as ocean crust that was accreted or plastered against the ancient coastline of California, much like the dirt that accumulates in front of a bulldozer blade as it crosses a construction site. All this seafloor material that was scraped off and added to the overlying plate was simultaneously

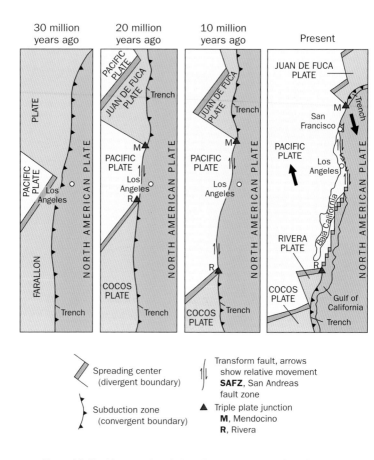

Figure 12. The history and evolution of the Farallon Plate from 30 million years ago to the present.

being uplifted and raised above sea level, to ultimately become part of the emerging California Coast Ranges (Figure 13).

Farther inland, a zone of volcanoes (the Cascades and older volcanoes whose roots are now exposed in the Sierra Nevada) began to emerge. Volcanoes, such as Mt. Shasta, Mt. Lassen, Mount Mazama (Crater Lake), Mount Hood,

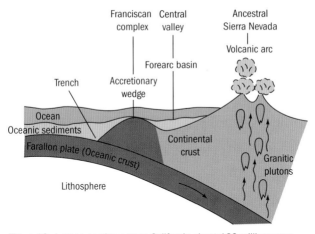

Figure 13. A cross section across California about 100 million years ago when subduction was taking place and the Sierra Nevada was an active range of volcanoes.

St. Helens and Rainer, all form in areas landward of trenches in response to the partial melting of crustal material as it is heated in its descent into Earth's warmer interior and its subsequent rise and eruption as molten lava on Earth's surface.

By about 25 to 30 million years ago, the smaller offshore Farallon Plate was nearly completely consumed beneath the advancing North American Plate, and, for the first time, the very large Pacific Plate met the large North American Plate head-on. These two plates first met off Mexico, and then these two huge crustal slabs underwent a major readjustment in their motion. The collision that had been underway for millions of years, which had been responsible for the offshore trench, the Sierra Nevada, the Cascades, and the ancestral Central Valley, was terminated for the most part, and these large plates now began to move alongside one another as the San Andreas Fault was initiated. Over the subsequent 15 to 20 million years, that portion of California west of the San Andreas Fault, extending from San Diego to Cape Mendocino, and including most of California's coastal counties has moved northwest about an inch and a half per year, on average, relative to the rest of the state to the east (Figure 14). Thus, California is slowly being torn apart, and the small earthquakes that occur daily, as well as the larger

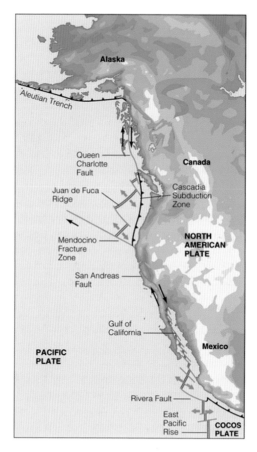

Figure 14. Western North America, showing how the San Andreas Fault forms the plate boundary between the North American and Pacific plates and how this transform boundary connects to ocean ridges to the north and south.

shocks that occur every 10 to 20 years, are evidence of the constant grinding along the boundary between the two massive slabs of Earth's crust. Assuming the present plate motion continues, western California will eventually drift off, albeit very slowly, and become the Madagascar of the North Pacific.

The striking features of California's diverse landscape, the San Andreas Fault and its associated earthquakes, the rugged coastal mountains, and the uplifted marine terraces and coastal cliffs that characterize much of the coastline, all have their origins in millions of years of large-scale tectonic processes that continue today. Subduction is still taking place off the coast of northern California, Oregon, and Washington. This process occasionally produces very large earthquakes and tsunamis, and also is responsible for the intermittently active volcanoes of the Cascade Range.

The rocks exposed along the coastline and in the sea cliffs provide evidence of this complex geological history and the changes the landscape has undergone. Much of the low, cliffed coastline between San Diego and Santa Barbara, and from Monterey to Half Moon Bay, consists of young, relatively weak sedimentary rocks, such as sandstones, mudstones, and shales, which were originally deposited in a relatively shallow offshore marine environment (Figure 15). These sedimentary rocks with their fossil shells and whalebones provide evidence for this area formerly being below sea level. In striking contrast, the Big Sur coast and much of the coastline north of San Francisco is dominated by steep cliffs and rocks of very different origin. Hard, volcanic materials, cherts, and a variety of rocks that were formed in an offshore trench were scraped off the subducted slab and then accreted to the continent during the millions of years of plate collision that dominate these rugged areas (Figure 16). These rocks are all part of a giant tectonic jigsaw puzzle that has slowly been assembled over many millions of years.

Figure 15. Steep sea cliff with caves at the base along the coast of San Mateo County. Photo Gary Griggs.

Figure 16. Tightly folded cherts exposed in the Marin Headlands just north of the Golden Gate Bridge. Photo Gary Griggs.

It would be difficult to find a coastline anywhere in the world that has had a more complex geological history than California's. It is because of the vastly differing rock types and regional geological histories that different sections of the state's coastline look so distinct. Some rocks are so hard and resistant that photographs taken of the coast 50 years ago look identical to those of today. Elsewhere, however, coastal bluff materials are so soft and weak that the coast is being eroded at rates of five feet or more each year, and these changes are easily recognized in comparing historical photographs (Figure 17).

Although large-scale coastal landforms, such as mountains, uplifted terraces, and sea cliffs, owe their relief and origin to regional tectonic events, surface processes, such as wave attack, rainfall and runoff, and landslides or other mass down-slope movements have subsequently altered them all. In addition, sea level along the coast has changed continuously through time such that the position of the shoreline is only a temporary one. Although these changes are not rapid, it is clear from historical photographs and geological evidence that the shoreline undergoes constant change. There is every reason to believe that the processes that have shaped the coastline in the past will continue far into the future, and, thus, our coastline will always be a work in progress.

Making Sense of the Landscape: The Distribution of Coastal Landforms

One way to help us understand why particular sections of coastline look so different is to break down the state's coastal areas into some distinct and recognizable landforms. One straightforward approach is to think of any particular part of California's coast as consisting of either (1) steep coastal mountains and sea cliffs with hundreds of feet of

A

Figure 17A. Arch near Steamer Lane along West Cliff Drive in Santa Cruz about 1887. Photo courtesy of Special Collections, University Library, University of California Santa Cruz.

B

Figure 17B. Site of arch in 2006. Photo Gary Griggs.

Figure 18. Steep coastal cliffs along the Big Sur coastline near Mill Creek. Photo Kenneth and Gabrielle Adelman, California Coastal Records Project, www.CaliforniaCoastline.org.

relief (Figure 18); (2) uplifted nearly horizontal marine terraces and lower sea cliffs and bluffs varying from 20 to perhaps 200 feet in height (Figure 19); and (3) low-relief shoreline areas with beaches, sand dunes, estuaries, or lagoons (Figure 20). As soon as we make up a coastal classification or a series of pigeonholes, however, we almost immediately recognize that there are transitional or intermediate areas that fall between the others, and that is fine. Beginning to recognize these distinct landforms helps us to understand how and why different parts of the coast look like they do today.

The great majority (72 percent, or about 790 miles) of the California coast consists of actively eroding sea cliffs. Of the state's 790 miles of cliffed coastline, about 650 miles consists of lower-relief cliffs and bluffs, typically eroded into marine terraces; the other 140 miles consists of high-relief cliffs and coastal mountains. The remaining 310 miles, or 28 percent, of the coastline is of low relief and relatively flat. These are the wide beaches and sand dunes, as well as the bays, estuaries,

Figure 19. The very wide lowest marine terrace near San Simeon. Photo Kenneth and Gabrielle Adelman, California Coastal Records Project, www.CaliforniaCoastline.org.

Figure 20. Tijuana slough and sand bars south of Imperial Beach in San Diego County. Photo Kenneth and Gabrielle Adelman, California Coastal Records Project, www.CaliforniaCoastline.org.

lagoons, and wetlands, which form many of the state's coastal recreational environments and parkland.

Steep Cliffs and Rugged Mountains

The state's high-relief, steep cliffs and coastal mountains are predominantly in northern and central California from Del Norte to Mendocino County, at the Marin Headlands just north of the Golden Gate, from Pacifica to Montara in San Mateo County, and along the Big Sur coast of Monterey and San Luis Obispo counties. High-relief, cliffed areas and rocky headlands are also along the Santa Monica Mountains coast. Because these spectacular areas are so hard to access and develop, they provide some of California's most pristine coastal scenery. Only limited development has taken place along these steep coastlines, and most of the mountainous areas are now protected within national forests and state parks.

These rugged stretches of coast typically consist of older, more resistant rock types and include granite, as well as the Franciscan Formation, a mélange or chaotic and folded mixture of sedimentary and volcanic rocks. These rocks tend to be much harder, and, as a result, are very resistant to erosion and form many of the protruding headlands or points along the state's coastline. Along the northern California coast, Point St. George, Trinidad Head, and Point Delgada are all Franciscan Formation outcrops (Figure 21). Bodega Head, Point Reyes, Point Piños, Point Cypress, and Point Lobos on the central coast all consist of granite. Proceeding further south, Point Sur, Point San Martin, Piedras Blancas, and Point San Luis are all Franciscan Formation exposures (Figure 22). These rock types erode very slowly, but, as in some parts of the Franciscan, may also be subject to large-scale landsliding or slumping, as along the Big Sur and Sonoma coastlines.

The steep topography of the Big Sur coast presented a major obstacle to overland travel from the time of the early

Figure 21. Trinidad Head, a prominent headland in Humboldt County. Photo Kenneth and Gabrielle Adelman, California Coastal Records Project, www.CaliforniaCoastline.org.

Figure 22. Point Lobos State Reserve south of Carmel. Photo Kenneth and Gabrielle Adelman, California Coastal Records Project, www. CaliforniaCoastline.org.

Spanish explorers until State Hwy. I was finally blasted through the solid rock in the late 1920s and 1930s. Today, this highway still clings precariously to the rocky cliffs. This narrow ribbon of access is a thrilling driving experience that traverses an otherwise mostly virgin coastline rising 5,000 feet to the crest of the Santa Lucia Mountains. Maintaining this highway remains a challenge, and the road is frequently closed in the winter months. Following the heavy rainfall of the 1982 and 1983 winters, the Big Sur coast was closed for about eight months until massive amounts of rock and soil could be removed from the roadway (Figure 23), hillsides could be reshaped and stabilized, and Hwy. I could be completely rebuilt. Each heavy winter brings new hillside failures and road closures in this rugged area.

Figure 23. A very large landslide initiated by heavy rainfall closed the Big Sur Highway for months during the 1983 winter and was subsequently repaired at a cost of over $7 million. Photo Gary Griggs.

Figure 24. Jade Cove along the Big Sur Coast of Monterey County. Photo Kenneth and Gabrielle Adelman, California Coastal Records Project, www.CaliforniaCoastline.org.

Topography here is so steep that there is little area for beaches to form and there is not a lot of sand-sized material available. The existing beaches often occur at the mouths of the coastal streams or are generally quite small and often very coarse-grained. Jade Cove, along the Big Sur coast, is an example of one of these rocky coves where visitors often find jade (Figure 24), the name commonly used for the rocks jadeite or nephrite. These are very resistant, green metamorphic rocks commonly found in the Franciscan Formation that outcrop in the local sea cliffs. Jade fragments have been eroded from the cliffs as well as from the nearshore area and have then been tumbled and polished by the waves, often ending up on the beach.

Level Playing Fields: Uplifted Marine Terraces

The coastline of California has many excellent examples of elevated marine terraces, which are characteristic features

Figure 25. A flight of five elevated marine terraces is preserved on the north coast of Santa Cruz County, although only three are easily distinguished. Photo Kenneth and Gabrielle Adelman, California Coastal Records Project, www.CaliforniaCoastline.org.

of collisional tectonic coasts where uplift has taken place. These flat benches, which typically resemble a massive flight of stairs, are usually less than a mile in width and commonly rise to elevations of 500 to 600 feet above sea level or higher (Figure 25). Each terrace consists of a nearly horizontal or gently seaward-sloping, eroded platform backed by a steep or degraded, relict sea cliff along its inland edge. The terraces were formed by wave erosion in the surf zone in the geological past, in essentially the same way as the rocky, intertidal platform, visible during low tides, is being eroded by breaking waves in the surf zone today.

Terraces exposed along the coast of California range from a single one, underlying the north coast town of Mendocino (Figure 26) and the University of California at Santa Barbara campus on the central coast, to as many as five along the north coast of Santa Cruz County, and

Figure 26. The picturesque town of Mendocino is built on the lowest coastal terrace. Photo Kenneth and Gabrielle Adelman, California Coastal Records Project, www.CaliforniaCoastline.org.

up to 13 on the Palos Verdes peninsula of Los Angeles County, culminating at an elevation of 1,480 feet. Nowhere along the entire coast of the United States is a more complete sequence of terraces preserved. Once a rancho of the Sepulveda family in the late 1800s, the Palos Verdes peninsula was developed as an elegant community in the 1920s, designed in part by the great landscape architect, Frederick Law Olmsted, who also designed New York City's Central Park.

Unfortunately for homeowners, the Palos Verdes peninsula's south coast proved to be geologically unstable. Cracks and broken windows that began to appear in some houses in 1956 were an early warning of pending disaster. Three years later, nearly 150 homes were completely destroyed when 300 acres of coastal hillside begin sliding slowly towards the shoreline on a slippery, lubricated layer of clay. The entire failure area was part of a much larger,

Figure 27. The large Portuguese Bend landslide on the Palos Verdes peninsula damaged and destroyed many homes. Photo Bruce Perry, CSUMB Geological Sciences.

1,000-acre ancient landslide that had been mapped by the U.S. Geological Survey, but developers and homebuyers alike ignored the well-publicized report with tragic consequences (Figure 27). Although a few houses survived this unusual 500- to 600-foot downhill journey, the end result was about $79 million (in 2008 dollars) in damage. The catalyst to failure in the now infamous Portuguese Bend Landslide was eventually identified as an excess of groundwater from heavy rainfall coupled with the infiltration from septic tanks, cesspools, and landscape irrigation.

About 20 years later, in the adjacent Abalone Cove, another part of this ancient landslide began moving. Cracks in the streets were again the first indication of deep-seated problems beneath the homes. About 80 acres, 25 homes, and 1,200 feet of shoreline were involved in this incident. Excess water was again named as the culprit along with a road that had been graded across the hillside. A series of wells were drilled in order to lower the water table in an effort to stabilize the slide.

Where multiple terraces are exposed, we can observe the preserved record of many previous sea level high stands that have been superimposed on a slowly, but continuously, rising coastline. Every terrace represents a warm climatic period or interglacial epoch, when ice caps and glaciers melted and sea level rose in response. Each of these climatic events was recorded as the waves eroded back the coastline, leaving a rocky intertidal terrace or bench. Along the California coast, where uplift has dominated the tectonic history for millions of years, these successive terraces have been gradually raised above sea level and preserved as ancient stairsteps along the coastal landscape.

Each newly formed terrace was exposed as sea level dropped in response to the onset of a new Ice Age. Beach sands and gravels first began to cover the bedrock platform as the ocean receded, often followed by the formation of sand dunes and, perhaps, stream derived sediments some time later. Over tens and hundreds of thousands of years, soils began to form and vegetation was established, a characteristic of the undisturbed marine terraces we see today. More commonly, however, these flat benches are now covered with homes, or entire communities, as well as farms, and they also form an ideal route for State Hwy. 1. Where the sea cliff has been eroded into an uplifted terrace, ancient beach and dune sediments, as well as the overlying darker soils, can be seen at the top of the sea cliff and record the past 100,000 years of deposition. One can often observe a preserved layer of fossil mollusks that bored down into the bedrock when the terrace was being formed; the layer is now exposed 25 to 50 feet above the present-day shoreline and beach (Figure 28).

How long ago did these marine terraces form? Dating these materials has been challenging. With the exception of the lowest or youngest terrace, leaching and dissolution

Figure 28. Mollusks are preserved in the first marine terrace along the central California coast. Photo Ian Miller.

by rain and ground water has removed most of the fossil remains. Mollusk shells from the lowest marine terrace are commonly exposed in the sea cliffs, but conventional carbon-14 dating is of little use because most of the shells are far older than the 50,000-year limit of this dating technique. Several other dating techniques have recently been used, and these have provided ages ranging from about 65,000 to about 500,000 years for the entire sequence of terraces along the state's coastline. So the terraces are young, geologically speaking, but they all formed long before any human habitation of California.

Low bluffs or cliffs cut into these uplifted marine terraces, which typically consist of sedimentary rocks such as shales, mudstones, and sandstones, characterize much of the coastline of San Diego, Orange, Santa Barbara, San Luis Obispo, Santa Cruz, and San Mateo counties. Along the northern California coast, portions of the Sonoma, Mendocino, Humboldt, and Del Norte coasts also expose uplifted

Figure 29. Sea Ranch is developed on the marine terrace of Sonoma County. Photo Kenneth and Gabrielle Adelman, California Coastal Records Project, www.CaliforniaCoastline.org.

marine terraces. The small, north-coast communities of Fort Bragg and Mendocino, for example, are built on uplifted coastal terraces, as is the Sea Ranch development in Sonoma County (Figure 29). Much of the coastline from Half Moon Bay in San Mateo County southward to northern Monterey Bay is also eroded into uplifted marine terraces, as are the Cambria, Cayucos and Morro Bay areas of the south-central coast.

The distribution of these nearly horizontal marine terraces has enabled California's intensive coastal development to take place. The communities from San Juan Capistrano to Camp Pendleton and from Oceanside south to Del Mar have all been built on the lowest and most extensive terrace. While slowly being replaced by homes and other development, the terraces, historically, were also used for agriculture: brussels sprouts and artichokes along the

Figure 30. The first marine terrace on Wilder Ranch State Park north of Santa Cruz stretches for nearly a mile from the sea cliff to State Hwy. 1. In the background two additional higher terraces can be seen. Photo Gary Griggs.

Santa Cruz coast (Figure 30) and avocados and citrus in Santa Barbara, for example. Ease of access and construction attracted developers, and the past 50 years saw the subdivision of thousands of acres of marine terraces in southern California.

Unfortunately, however, the weak sedimentary rocks that lent themselves to wave erosion, resulting in the formation of these terraces in the geological past, are the same materials exposed in the coastal cliffs today. These rocks are very susceptible to erosion by waves, as well as by rainfall, runoff, and landslides, and thus they continue to retreat landward (Figure 31). Continued global warming with the associated melting of ice caps and rising sea level will progressively move these weak bluffs and cliffs landward over time. This has and will continue to present challenges to those communities and landowners who have developments or homes on these slowly retreating features.

Figure 31. Student apartments built at the edge of the lowest marine terrace near the University of California Santa Barbara are threatened by cliff retreat. Photo Kenneth and Gabrielle Adelman, California Coastal Records Project, www.CaliforniaCoastline.org.

Next to the Rising Tide: Beaches, Bays and Estuaries

A little over 300 miles of the state's coastline is of low relief and consists of sandy beaches, occasionally backed by sand dunes, or may actually be below sea level and covered with water, including bays, estuaries, lagoons, and other wetlands. Much of the Los Angeles County shoreline falls into this category, including the broad beaches of Santa Monica and Redondo Beach and the Ballona Creek wetlands. Beaches backed by bays, lagoons, and wetlands, rather than cliffs or terraces, characterize the area between Long Beach and Newport Beach. Several of these bays or lagoons have been converted to popular waterfront communities with boat access, such as Alamitos Bay and Huntington Harbor.

Most low-relief areas along the coast are the broad flood-plains and channels of the rivers and streams that originate in the coastal mountains and deposited sediments over hundreds of thousands of years. Some streams are quite small, so that their channels and floodplains are narrow and the beaches at their mouths are limited in extent. The Russian River, the San Lorenzo River, the Big Sur River, and Malibu Creek are several examples. Other streams, owing to the size of the drainages or to the low relief near their mouths, have built wide floodplains. In southern California, these have been completely urbanized. The Los Angeles Basin, now home to perhaps 10 million people, was formed by the combined floodplains of the Los Angeles, San Gabriel, and Santa Ana rivers. Because of channelization, dams, reservoirs, water withdrawals, sand and gravel mining, and other alterations, these rivers bear little resemblance to the original channels of 150 years ago (Figure 32). These rivers once delivered millions of cubic yards of sand to the shoreline, which, historically, nourished the beaches of the Santa Monica Bay, as well as those between Long Beach and Newport Beach.

Figure 32. The Los Angeles River is a concrete channel where it enters the completely industrialized Port of Long Beach. Photo Bruce Perry, CSUMB Geological Sciences.

The mouths of many coastal rivers or streams, however, are now bays, lagoons, or estuaries. During the low sea levels of the glacial periods, California's streams traversed the exposed continental shelf, eroding deep canyons or channels, and discharged five to 25 miles farther to the west. Each time an Ice Age ended, glaciers retreated and ice caps melted causing a rise in sea level, usually of several hundred feet. As sea level rose, the streams migrated back across the shelf, and, today, in a climatically warm or interglacial period, sea level is higher than it has been for about the last 120,000 years. The mouths of most coastal streams have been drowned or flooded by the high sea level, forming lagoons or estuaries. Sediment carried by the streams has been deposited and reworked by wave action and wind into sand spits and dunes and, in some cases, altered by engineering. Humboldt Bay, Bolinas Lagoon, and Morro Bay (Figure 33) are good examples, as are those many coastal lagoons of southern California, such as Mugu Lagoon, Batiquitos Lagoon, Aqua

Figure 33. The community of Stinson Beach was built on the sand spit separating Bolinas Lagoon from the ocean. Photo Kenneth and Gabrielle Adelman, California Coastal Records Project, www.CaliforniaCoastline.org.

Figure 34. Huntington Beach with the Huntington Harbour development built around a former wetland. Photo Kenneth and Gabrielle Adelman, California Coastal Records Project, www.CaliforniaCoastline.org.

Hedionda Lagoon, Balboa Bay, and San Diego Bay. Other lagoon areas have been completely altered by filling and reclamation, so that they no longer bear much resemblance to their original character and configuration: Marina del Rey, Huntington Harbor, Balboa Bay, and Mission Bay are good examples (Figure 34).

The Golden Gate and San Francisco Bay represent a major break in the otherwise steep cliffs and mountains that make up the adjacent coastline to the north and south. The bay itself is a large, depressed block that lies between the San Andreas Fault to the west and the Hayward Fault to the east, but is now mostly covered with seawater (Figure 35). The bay we see today is actually quite young geologically; it is the estuary where the outflow of the San Joaquin and Sacramento rivers meets the salty waters of the Pacific Ocean. These rivers, together, drain about 40 percent of the state's entire land area. The Golden Gate is a recent discharge point, probably only formed within the past 600,000 to 700,000 years.

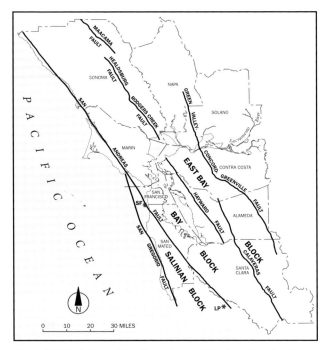

Figure 35. The faults and locations of major historic earthquakes in the San Francisco Bay area. SF = 1906 San Francisco earthquake epicenter. LP = 1989 Loma Prieta earthquake epicenter.

Prior to that time the rivers draining the vast Central Valley probably cut through the Coast Ranges and discharged near the present Monterey Bay.

As sea level has risen and fallen over the past 600,000 years, in response to glacial and interglacial periods, the ocean periodically re-entered the Golden Gate and filled the Bay, creating an estuary where fresh and salt water mixed, only to drain again when sea level dropped. During low sea levels, the combined Sacramento and San Joaquin rivers cut a channel through the Golden Gate that is now over 350 feet below sea level. The vast volumes of sand carried by strong tidal flows through the Golden Gate in recent years have

TABLE 1 Classification of Sediments by Size

Size Designation	Diameter in Millimeters
Boulders	>256
Cobbles	64 to 256
Pebbles	4 to 64
Granules	2 to 4
Very Coarse Sand	1 to 2
Coarse Sand	0.5 to 1
Medium Sand	0.25 to 0.5
Fine Sand	0.125 to 0.250
Very Fine Sand	0.0625 to 0.125
Silt	0.004 to 0.0625

formed some of the largest sea floor sand waves observed anywhere on Earth.

Coastal Sand Piles

There is something about sand dunes that appeals to all of us—mountains of white sand we can climb up and roll or run down. But why does sand accumulate in these huge piles at some well-known locations, such as Pismo Beach or Sand City in southern Monterey Bay? We do not, however, find dunes or, at least, large dunes, along most beaches.

The formation of large sand dunes requires a lot of fine-grained sand. Geologists and others who study sand or sediment have developed a simple system (Table 1) that breaks down or classifies sediment by increasing grain size, such as clay, silt, sand, pebbles, cobbles, and boulders. But even sand is distinguished as very fine-grained, fine-grained, medium-grained, and so forth. Wind is a very effective agent for moving sand around, but, generally, the sand has to be fine-grained in order for wind to move enough sand to form dunes.

Most of the sand on our beaches and in the dunes came originally from rivers and streams that discharge along the state's shoreline. At the mouths of the streams where the sand has been deposited, waves take over the workload and begin to further sort out sand and move it along the shoreline. Once enough sand accumulates, a few more conditions are necessary before we can form extensive dunes. The shoreline topography has to be of low relief so that a wide beach can form. When enough sand has been built up on the berm or back-beach, the place you would typically spread out your towel in summer, and there is a reasonably consistent onshore wind, the beach sand can begin to be blown onshore or inland, away from the beach. The wind, however, needs to blow in a persistently onshore direction. Also needed is a low-lying or low-relief area landward of the beach where the sand can be transported and accumulate. If the beach is narrow or high cliffs or bluffs back the beach, which is the case along about 70 percent of California's coastline, dunes cannot form or migrate.

During the last Ice Age, one of many which occurred during the Pleistocene epoch, sea level was about 350 to 400 feet lower than today along the coast of California, and the shoreline was far to the west. You could walk out to the Farallon Islands off of the Golden Gate and never get your feet wet. Indeed, this was a time when early humans may have entered California by migrating down the then exposed continental shelf after crossing from Siberia via the land bridge across the Bering Straits. As sea level rose and fell repeatedly throughout the Pleistocene, in response to global warming and cooling, the ice caps and glaciers contracted and expanded, and the beach moved back and forth across the continental shelf many times. Where large rivers were present and the shelf was wide, vast areas of sand were left behind as ancient beaches. When the wind blew, it had miles of sand to work with. Some of our largest sand dunes, such as those in southern Monterey Bay (Figure 36), had

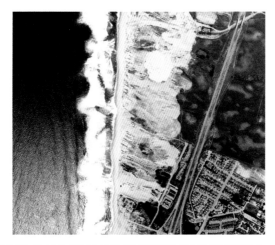

Figure 36. Sand dunes of southern Monterey Bay. Photo California Department of Boating and Waterways.

their origins under these Ice Age conditions. What we see today is only a small remnant of what was probably a much more extensive system of dunes that was exposed 15,000 to 20,000 years ago, when sea level was lower.

Sand is held in place on the beach by gravity, or the weight of the individual grains, and by the friction between grains. These two factors allow sand to maintain a natural angle of repose or a stable slope of about 30 to 35 degrees. However, if we wet the sand, there is additional cohesion or bonding between the grains that allows them to stand at a much steeper, even vertical, slope. You can build an elaborate sand castle with wet sand, but dry sand just doesn't work.

In order for the wind to begin to move sand on a dry beach, the velocity has to exert enough force on the individual grains to overcome both gravity and the friction between the grains. As the wind picks up speed, the sand grains will gradually begin to start moving, and soon it may be too

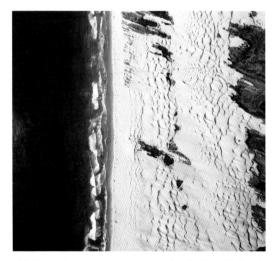

Figure 37. Extensive sand dunes at Pismo Beach. Photo California Department of Boating and Waterways.

uncomfortable to be lying on the sand. Sand grains blown by the wind can move by rolling or bouncing along the surface, or, as the wind increases in velocity, individual grains can be lifted up off the surface and become airborne for short hops, a process called saltation. Where the wind is blowing strongly, sediment can be picked up and suspended to form dust clouds and transported for miles. This is what happened during the Great Depression, when the Midwest farmland became known as "the Dust Bowl." Normally, however, wind velocity is not high enough for a long enough period of time to move sand in suspension for any great distance.

Where dunes migrate inland, they are removing sand more or less permanently from the beach. In the Pismo Dunes area of the central coast, about 200,000 cubic yards of sand are blown inland annually along the 35-mile coastline from Pismo Beach to Point Arguello (Figure 37). This is the equivalent of about 20,000 dump truck loads of sand lost from the beach

each year. While the original source of sand for many of California's large dunes is clear, the origin of the sand that formed the Pismo and Nipomo dunes is not all that obvious. There are no large rivers in the immediate vicinity at the present time, so we have to think farther back in time when conditions were probably quite different than today.

More than half of the city of San Francisco, from Ocean Beach to the Bay, was once covered with sand dunes (Figure 38). The original source of the sand was the Sierra Nevada, far to the east. Sand was brought down the Sacramento and San Joaquin rivers, carried through the Bay, and ultimately reached the shoreline at Ocean Beach. Sand was then blown from the beach across present day Golden Gate Park and built dunes as high as 60 feet, all now buried beneath the present houses and streets of San Francisco.

Along the far north coast, extensive dunes occur north of Crescent City and along both the north and south spits of Humboldt Bay. The Smith, Mad, and Eel rivers were the likely sand sources for these dunes. To the south, Point Reyes and southern Monterey Bay between Moss Landing and Monterey are underlain by sand dunes. The sand spit at Morro Bay, the Oxnard Plain, the shoreline from Santa Monica to El Segundo, and the Silver Strand from Coronado to the Mexican Border are also sites of well-developed coastal sand dunes, although covered by development in many places.

Dunes are important coastal buffers because they are flexible barriers to storm waves and provide protection to the lower-lying back-dune areas. In fact, wherever dunes can be created and stabilized, they often work better than seawalls. Dunes also maintain a large stockpile of sand that feeds the beach during severe storms or prolonged periods of wave attack. Under storm assault, the beach is first cut back and, if wave erosion continues, portions of the frontal dune may be eroded. This sand is moved offshore, where it is stored in sand bars that tend to reduce the wave energy impinging on the shoreline, because the waves will break farther

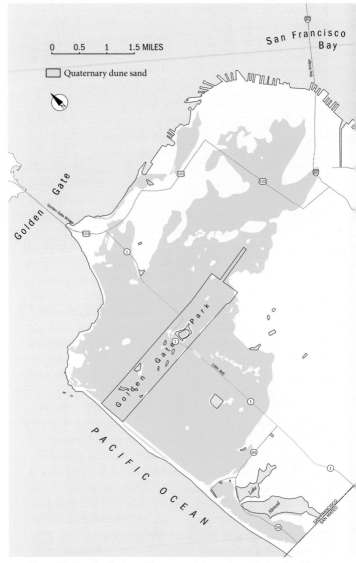

Figure 38. The distribution of former sand dunes beneath the city of San Francisco (shown in yellow), now completely buried under development.

Figure 39. Erosion of the frontal dune at Pajaro Dunes during the El Niño winter of 1983 threatened many homes. A one-mile-long riprap revetment was subsequently built to protect the homes. Photo Gary Griggs.

offshore. As the winter storms subside, smaller spring and summer waves transport sand back onto the beach, which will ultimately be rebuilt. With time or the absence of large storms, the excess sand will be moved onshore by wind and will rebuild the dunes again. The process of natural dune rebuilding may take several years. Dune erosion, either during storms or because of a reduction in sand supply, can be destructive to any structures built on the dunes (Figure 39).

Sand dunes must be seen as ephemeral or temporary landforms. Storms will recur, sandbars will shift, and dunes will erode, rebuild, and migrate. In addition, dune instability may result from human impacts in the form of construction or recreation. The primary, frontal, or fore dune is particularly prone to change, as has been discovered in recent years by owners of new condominiums and houses perched on active sand dunes. After many years of observations, landscape architect Ian McHarg recommended decades ago in his classic book, *Design with Nature,* that no development, recreation, or human activity of any type occur on the primary or secondary dunes, which are the least stable and contain the most fragile vegetation. This principle was widely violated along the California coast in the past, with costly consequences. Development, if it is to occur at all, should take place in the back dune area, which has the advantage of protection from winter storms, but the disadvantage of not providing ocean views.

Recreational impact in sand dune areas has historically been widespread, mainly from pedestrian traffic and off-road vehicle use. Most foot traffic impacts come from uncontrolled crossings from the back dune area to the beach. Heavy foot traffic decreases the amount of vegetation, which in turn accelerates dune destabilization and migration. Off-road vehicle traffic, which is a common recreational practice in some dune areas, has the same effects—loss of vegetation and destabilization of the dunes—which are difficult to repair. The fragile nature of sand dunes is now more widely appreciated than in the past, and more attention is paid to proposals that would remove vegetation, lower groundwater levels, or breach the dunes themselves. Restricted and fenced pathways, boardwalks and re-vegetation, as well as sand fences, particularly in our coastal parks, are paying off by protecting vegetation and thereby aiding dune stabilization.

From Rain Forest to Desert: An Introduction to California's Coastal Climate

Rain forest to desert pretty well summarizes the climatic differences along California's 1,100-mile coastline. Los Angeles, Orange and San Diego counties, at one extreme, are essentially deserts that would have you believe that they are not. In a good year, they get about 10 to 12 inches of rain and, before development and the importation of water, were characterized by an arid landscape with only sparse chaparral vegetation (Figure 40). It was not really a place that welcomed visitors, much less invited the growth of a huge metropolitan area. The tropical landscaping in some southern California coastal neighborhoods today looks more like Hawaii than southern California, and it is all dependent upon imported water. Most local streams carry water for only a few months of the year or after heavy rainstorms,

Figure 40. The arid southern California landscape at Camp Pendleton, northern San Diego County. Photo Kenneth and Gabrielle Adelman, California Coastal Records Project, www.CaliforniaCoastline.org.

which can produce flash floods that come and go in a matter of a few hours. Many downstream portions of these rivers have now been completely urbanized and replaced by concrete flood control channels, which have eliminated any semblance of the original riparian corridors (Figure 32). Gone are the sycamores and willows, replaced by concrete walls and chain link fences.

At the other extreme, Eureka lies in the heavily redwood-forested North Coast Ranges, where rainfall often exceeds 50 to 75 inches per year (Figure 41). This is where most of the state's large rivers are located and where most of the fresh water, and also sediment, are discharged. The storms bringing the rainfall are often the same storms that bring the waves that break on the shoreline; they are both strongly seasonal, with the highest rainfall and the largest storm waves typically concentrated between December and March. The climate for much of California's coastal areas undergoes clear seasonal

Figure 41. The redwood forested coastline of Redwood Creek National Park in Humboldt County. Photo Kenneth and Gabrielle Adelman, California Coastal Records Project, www.CaliforniaCoastline.org.

changes, although compared to the Midwest or New England, southern California has very mild winters. Transplanted immigrants from New York or Chicago claim that the coast of California doesn't really have winters for there are no ice storms, salted roadways, or frozen ponds.

California's Coastal Climate: An Almost Endless Summer

It has been said that climate is what we predict and weather is what we get, and there is some truth in this. The weather along California's coast, including storms, precipitation, and waves, is directly related to the changing seasonal patterns of oceanic and atmospheric circulation within and above the Pacific Ocean. Perhaps the most important factor affecting what happens along the coast in any particular month and at any specific location is the behavior of one large mass of air, the North Pacific High. This dominating feature forms as air that has been warmed by solar heating near the equator rises and moves northward toward the polar region. As this air rises, it cools in the upper atmosphere. Some cool air sinks toward the ocean surface, forming a column of dense air and, therefore, high atmospheric pressure several thousand miles north of the equator.

The North Pacific High (so named because of the high atmospheric pressure resulting from this cool, descending air mass) is an active feature, and it moves north and south according to seasonal variations in the amount of solar energy Earth receives. During the Northern Hemisphere spring and summer, as the area of maximum heating moves north due to the tilt of Earth on its axis towards the sun, the high will migrate north, typically to about the latitude of San Francisco (38 degrees north). During winter, when the Northern Hemisphere is tilted away from the sun, the area of maximum heating moves south. In response, the

North Pacific High migrates south to about the latitude of the Hawaiian Islands (20 degrees north).

The North Pacific High varies in size, strength, and relative atmospheric pressure from year to year. How far north or offshore it reaches, as well as how far inland it migrates over western North America, can also fluctuate. Although these variations in position and strength are unpredictable from year to year, we know that they exert a strong influence on California's coastal climate, affecting storm track direction and location and, therefore, precipitation distribution, as well as the wave energy that batters the coastline (Figure 42).

The summer climate of the California coast is strongly influenced by the strength and position of the North Pacific High. The high-pressure area offshore either breaks down the large storms moving east from the western Pacific or deflects them northward towards Oregon and Washington so that they miss the California coast altogether (Figure 42). This is why rainfall along the coastline of California is usually very low or completely lacking in the summer months and occurs only when the high is displaced far to the south or weakens enough to allow storms to move over the coast. During the winter months, however, when the North Pacific High weakens and moves southward, our protection disappears, and large storms forming in the western Pacific impact us directly, along with precipitation and large waves. It is useful to understand that we get storms from different areas of the Pacific Ocean, and that they each affect the coastline differently.

The most common type of storm reaching California originates in low-pressure areas south of the Aleutian Islands and advances from the northwest down the coast. These are powerful storms, particularly along California's northern coast, and may generate 20 to 30-foot-high waves offshore and also high winds. Waves from these storms usually approach from the northwest and impact both

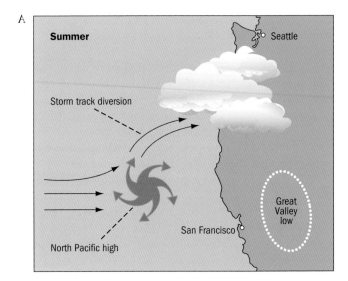

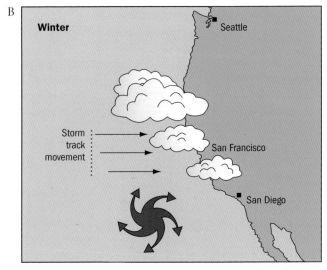

Figure 42. Atmospheric circulation and the position of the North Pacific High during the (A) summer, and (B) winter.

the sea cliffs and the beaches, driving littoral currents and sand on the shoreline southward along most of the state's coast.

The historical record of storm damage along California's coast tells us that periods of greatest erosion and damage correspond to times when very large waves and high tides occurred simultaneously. Severe storms of this type occurred in December 1940 and again in January 1941, causing considerable damage along the entire coast, particularly the central and south coast. In December 1977 and January 1978, the north and central coast experienced severe storms, elevated sea levels, and shoreline damage. The greatest coastal storm damage in 50 years occurred during the first three months of 1983, when a number of large waves reached the coastline coincident with high tides and elevated sea levels from a large El Niño (Figure 43). The storms of 1997–98 also had severe impacts on the state's coastline, although the construction of many new seawalls and emplacement of riprap following the 1982–83 winter tended to reduce the overall property damage.

Figure 43. Damage to beach-level homes on Beach Drive in Rio Del Mar, Santa Cruz County during the 1983 El Niño. Photo Gary Griggs.

Storms originating in the open Pacific often pass through the Hawaiian Islands area, where they pick up considerable moisture from the warm tropical waters. These are called the "Pineapple Express," and they approach the southern California coast from the west. Such storms were responsible for major damage to homes, piers, and roads along the southern California coast during the winters of 1977–78 and 1979–80. During these winters, high rainfall led to many coastal landslides, which greatly accelerated cliff erosion. When heavy rains arrive in winter, immediately following large brush fires such as those that regularly burn through the Santa Monica Mountains and also the Big Sur area, soil erosion and mud flows can deliver huge volumes of sediment from these now scorched and barren coastal watersheds to the shoreline.

Hurricane-generated storms create violent winds that approach California from the south, but occur in summer and early fall, rather than during the winter months. Such storms have rarely come to the California coast in recent years, but often devastate the coast of Baja California to the south before moving eastward or westward and dissipating. If this type of storm does reach southern California, it is generally accompanied by southerly winds and large waves that can be disastrous to south or southwest-facing coasts, such as Malibu, Newport, Laguna Beach, and Long Beach. Prior to 1983, the last hurricane-generated storm to reach the southern California coast occurred in September 1939. Despite the presence of groins, jetties, breakwaters, and other coastal structures, beaches were inundated and numerous homes and structures at Long Beach and Newport were destroyed or severely damaged in that storm.

Following the warm-water El Niño event of 1982–83 in the Pacific, storms of this type have become more frequent. The Hawaiian Islands were hit by such a storm (Hurricane Iniki) in November 1982, which left the most severe storm damage of the century on the island of Kauai. On January

17 and 18, 1988, a largely unforecast "southeaster" hit the coast of southern California with peak offshore wave heights of over 30 feet. Damage to oceanfront structures and infrastructure exceeded $44 million (in 2008 dollars), with the greatest damage occurring in Redondo Beach, Huntington Beach, and San Diego. Conditions were so bad that residents of the Portofino Inn, inside King Harbor in Redondo Beach, had to be rescued from the roof by helicopter.

El Niño and Interdecadal Climate Oscillations

What Is El Niño?

People in Peru have known for at least four centuries, and probably far longer, that the intrusion of a current of warm water from the west every few years leads to a dramatic reduction in the population of anchovies in coastal waters. This anchovy decline not only severely impacts the Peruvian fishing industry but also causes a decline in marine mammals and sea birds that rely on anchovies as a food source. In addition to the ecological impacts, this intrusion of warm water produces torrential rainfall in the coastal mountains accompanied by floods, mudflows, and landslides. Although the extra rainfall has a positive effect on agriculture in an otherwise dry coastal area, the large-scale, negative economic consequences of this event have been known for generations.

In Peru, because this warm-water phenomenon often arrived around Christmas, it was given the name El Niño, Spanish for "the child," in reference to the timing of the birth of Jesus. Over the past 30 years, we have learned a lot more about the global scale of this event, and its widespread and diverse impacts have been gradually understood and more fully appreciated. We now recognize that an El Niño event is linked to an alteration of atmospheric pressure systems over the equatorial Pacific called the Southern Oscillation. This large-scale phenomenon is now more accurately called El Niño—Southern Oscillation, or ENSO for short, and is characterized by major shifts in both atmospheric and oceanic circulation and also surface water temperatures throughout the entire Pacific basin.

In what are thought of as "normal" oceanographic conditions, trade winds over the Pacific blow towards the equator from the northeast and southeast. These regular winds move warm surface waters toward the western equatorial Pacific, where a large pool of warm water accumulates (Figure 44). The water leaving this warm pool flows both northward along the edge of Asia towards Japan (the Kuroshio Current) and also southward along the edge of Australia (the East-Australian Current). In both northern and southern hemispheres these currents then turn eastward and head back across the Pacific toward North and South America to complete their travels.

Every three to seven years, however, the normal atmospheric circulation system over the Pacific Ocean breaks down. For reasons we still don't completely understand, the

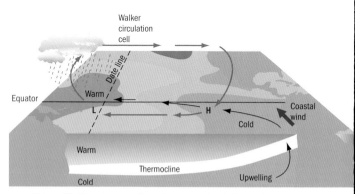

Figure 44. The atmospheric and oceanic circulation and water temperatures in the equatorial Pacific during normal conditions.

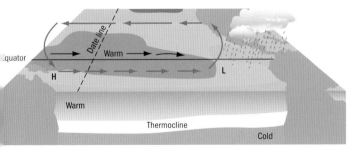

Figure 45. The atmospheric and oceanic circulation and water temperatures in the equatorial Pacific during El Niño conditions.

trade winds weaken, atmospheric pressures across the Pacific reverse, and winds begin to blow from west to east, moving the warm pool of water gradually back toward South America and initiating an El Niño (Figure 45). The size of the pool of warm water is usually a pretty good indicator of the magnitude of the ENSO event. Through the use of satellites and instrumented surface buoys, we can now accurately measure and monitor the size, temperature, and eastward movement of this pool of warm water. Because of this monitoring, NOAA and the National Weather Service circulated warnings and predictions of the large 1997–98 El Niño months in advance. There was a long time interval, however, between the initial oceanographic observations in spring, which suggested an El Niño was building in the western Pacific, and its ultimate arrival on the coast of California. Although the 1997–98 ENSO event was predicted quite accurately, the impact was not really felt until January and March of 1998, almost a year after the initial predictions. As a result, many coastal residents and state and local agencies concluded that this event simply was not going to take place as announced and took no particular precautions; some editorial cartoons even proclaimed the event as "El No Show." They were a little too impatient. When it did finally arrive, it struck with a vengeance.

It is important to realize that simply predicting a large disaster, whether a volcanic eruption, a flood, or the arrival of an El Niño, doesn't, in and of itself, eliminate or reduce the damage along the coastline. Our ability to successfully predict certain impending disasters, such as earthquakes, for example, is severely limited. We can do far better with rainstorms and floods. The value in any prediction is being able to take action well in advance that would help reduce the impacts and damage. If a large El Niño is predicted to hit the coast of California, accompanied by elevated sea levels and very large waves, there is not a whole lot we can do to significantly reduce the expected shoreline property damage (Figure 46). We can stack up sand bags in front of our oceanfront houses, board up the windows, and move our families to a safer location, but these are just short-term bandages in the big picture of things.

As this warm El Niño current moves eastward across the equatorial Pacific Ocean, it raises surface water temperatures enough to severely damage coral reefs. This has been a common occurrence in recent years, and large areas of coral have been decimated through what has been called coral bleaching

Figure 46. Storm waves hitting the cliffs along West Cliff Drive in Santa Cruz during the 1997–98 El Niño. Photo Gary Griggs.

in Tahiti, the Galapagos, and many other Pacific Islands. The bleaching results from the coral expelling their symbiotic algae, which may lead to the death of the coral.

When the warm surface water flowing eastward across the Pacific finally reaches the coast of Ecuador and Peru, it divides, moving both north and south along the coast as a large slow motion wave, raising regional sea levels slightly and transporting normally tropical species to more temperate waters. The large and voracious Humboldt squid that have been found in increasing numbers off the coast of California in recent years (Figure 47) is one good example of this species displacement in response to warmer water moving north. Although Humboldt Squid are generally found in the warm Pacific waters off the coast of Baja California, recent years have shown an increase in their northern migration. The large 1997–98 El Niño produced the first sightings of Humboldt

Figure 47. Growing up to six feet long, Humboldt squid are formidable predators that hunt krill and a variety of fishes. Their normal habitat is within tropical and subtropical waters of the Eastern Pacific. Over the last five years, however, Humboldt squid have begun moving into cooler water areas such as central California. © 2003 MBARI.

Squid in Monterey Bay. They returned to Monterey Bay during the minor El Niño event of 2002 in higher numbers and now appear to have become year-round residents. Similar trends have been observed farther north off the coasts of Washington, Oregon, and even Alaska, although there are not yet year-round Humboldt Squid populations in these locations.

Pacific Decadal Oscillations and the Coast of California

Our common perceptions about California's coastal climate, until fairly recently, were that it was a more or less a random phenomenon, and what happened each year was simply not possible to predict in advance. We had no way of knowing whether we could expect a very wet or a dry winter, and what the wave climate might be like. We had droughts in some years and intense rainfall in others, but there did not seem to be any recognizable or repeatable patterns. As more years of climate data have accumulated and our observations have been more carefully analyzed, some clear patterns have begun to emerge. We still cannot predict the weather very far in advance, nor do we completely understand what drives the changes, but we have recognized some clear and repeatable patterns in our climate.

Similar to the forces that drive the North Pacific High and that produce ENSO events, we now recognize a large-scale, Pacific Basin–wide set of conditions, which has been designated the Pacific Decadal Oscillation, or PDO for short. We can identify periods, typically lasting several decades, when the coastal climate and storm conditions are significantly different than during other decadal-length time periods (Figure 48). The Pacific Basin, including the ocean off of California, oscillates between what have been designated as warm and cool phases of the Pacific Decadal Oscillation. As ocean water temperatures rise, for example, during a warm or positive phase of the PDO, air temperatures also rise, which

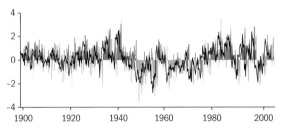

Figure 48. The Pacific Decadal Oscillation index from 1900 to 2004, with red indicating warm phase and blue indicating cool phase.

affects atmospheric pressures; ultimately, wind patterns and storm tracks are all affected. It turns out that El Niño events are much more frequent and severe during warm PDO cycles, which typically translate to warmer ocean water and higher sea levels, more rainfall and flooding, more frequent and vigorous coastal storms, and, as a result, greater beach and bluff erosion. These conditions also affect the oceanic life just offshore, where species are more abundant and tend to migrate elsewhere where conditions might be more favorable.

During a cooler (or negative) phase of the PDO, in contrast, La Niña events dominate. This means that cooler water, lower rainfall, and fewer large and damaging coastal storms give rise overall to a more benign climate along the California coast. The period from 1945 to 1977 was a negative or cool phase of the PDO, with La Niña conditions dominating (Figure 49). This was a period of generally calm weather for the California coast, which typically meant less precipitation and fewer damaging coastal storms. Conditions were attractive for oceanfront development, and this was precisely the time period when southern California's population exploded and much of the state's coastal construction took place. Land was subdivided, lots were created, and homes and other structures were built on the cliffs, bluffs, dunes, and on the back-beach.

About 1978, the Pacific shifted back to a warm or positive phase of the Pacific Decadal Oscillation, and, along with

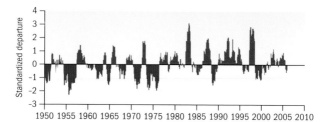

Figure 49. El Niño (red) and La Niña (blue) conditions from 1950 to 2005.

elevated sea levels from warmer water, the California coast was hit by some of the most damaging storms in several decades. Many oceanfront residents, planners, engineers, and public officials were surprised as private and public losses reached approximately $59 million (in 2008 dollars).

Five years later, high tides, elevated sea levels, and storm waves during the 1982–83 El Niño winter inflicted over $218 million (in 2008 dollars) in damage to California's shoreline. During the months of January, February, and March of 1983, eight major storms struck the coast accompanied by large waves. The arrival of large waves, unfortunately, tended to coincide with high tides, which further exacerbated the damage. Losses were widespread from north to south and not restricted to broken windows and flooding of low-lying areas; 33 oceanfront homes were totally destroyed and 3,000 homes and businesses were damaged. The elevated sea levels and large waves damaged breakwaters, piers, park facilities, seawalls, coastal infrastructure, and public and private structures (Figures 50 and 51). This event was a wake-up call for the entire coastline and made it clear that the California coast was not the endless summer we had been lulled into believing it was.

Again, in 1997–98, another major El Niño winter seriously impacted the state's coastline; more property was lost and more homes were damaged or destroyed. Although most

Figure 50. Storm waves combined with high tides and elevated sea levels led to the most severe coastal storm damage in 50 years along the entire coast of California during the 1983 El Niño. Photo Gary Griggs.

Figure 51. Large waves in northern Monterey Bay during the 1983 El Niño undermined the concrete slab of this beachfront house, which then slid into the water. Photo Gary Griggs.

oceanographic and meteorological indicators suggested that the 1997–98 ENSO disturbance was more intense than the 1982–83 event; the state's coastline suffered far less damage than in the earlier event. In 1997–98, the largest waves from the two biggest storms hit during lower periods in the monthly tidal cycles, significantly reducing the impact of the waves on the shoreline. Another important factor contributing to the disproportionate damage between the two winters was the higher percentage of shoreline that had been armored during the intervening 15 years. By the time the 1997–98 ENSO event arrived, most of the areas seriously damaged in the 1982–83 winter had been armored by substantial seawalls or revetments.

What has become clear is that California's coastal climate and storm activity is not completely random but that there are periods lasting several decades that are quite distinct. The frequency and magnitude of damaging coastal storms is greater during El Niño-dominated, warm PDO cycles than during cooler, La Niña-dominated cycles (Figure 49). This has been evident in hindsight from the California coastal-storm-damage history of the past 75 years. It initially appeared that in 2000 we transitioned into a cool PDO phase and that we might get some storm relief for several decades. However, oceanographic data from 2002 to 2007 indicate that we still are in a warm PDO phase, although the El Niño events have been very mild. The oceans and atmosphere are also continuing to warm, and we do not yet know with any certainty how a warmer climate and ocean will affect the frequency and intensity of future El Niño-events.

June Gloom: Coastal Fog and Why We Need It

While morning fog often comes as a surprise to June visitors to the beaches of southern California, long-term residents know and expect fog in the morning during the early summer

Figure 52. Fog is common along the California coast or just offshore during the spring and early summer months. Photo Jeremy Lezin, Ortalon Productions.

months (Figure 52). In San Diego, this phenomena is often referred to as "June gloom." I spent a summer as a college student life-guarding on the beach in Santa Barbara. Many of those mornings started out foggy and cool, and it was not until almost noon some days that the fog would finally lift and people would start to arrive at the beach, giving the lifeguards something to worry about. Living for some years now near the beach in Santa Cruz, I often wake up to early-morning, summer fog, which disappears as I drive uphill to the University campus.

Fog forms when water vapor in the air condenses and a large number of the droplets aggregate to form a visible mass, which may cover large areas along the coastline. These water droplets scatter the light, which makes visibility very poor near the ground. Fog can wreak havoc on transportation in coastal areas. San Diego's airport is often closed due to fog. For years, foghorns have warned ships traveling along California's coast in the fog of the presence of the rocks and other hazards along the coastline. Point Arguello, just north of Point Conception, has been the site of so many shipwrecks, because of the fog that surrounds this area, that it has been referred to as the "Graveyard of the Pacific." The U.S. Navy's greatest peacetime disaster occurred off Point Arguello on September 9, 1923, when seven destroyers followed each other onto the rocks in the fog (Figure 53).

Fog also has its benefits, however, particularly along the coast of northern California where the Coast Redwoods derive a significant portion of their water supply from fog drip. Fog is a fact of life for coastal redwoods and their very existence depends on it. Because summers are very dry in the Coast Ranges, moisture from fog is needed to maintain tree health through these months. The foliage of the redwoods literally strips the moisture out of the coastal fog and this moisture can provide as much as 40 to 45 percent of their annual water uptake.

Figure 53. Heavy fog along the central coast at Point Honda led to seven destroyers running aground on the evening of September 8, 1923. Photo United States Navy.

There are different coastal conditions that can generate fog, and California experiences these frequently in summer, to our beach-going visitor's dismay. Coastal fog often occurs in the summer months when moist air that has been heated over the land during the day moves out over the cold waters of the California Current in the evening, and allows the moisture to condense. When the moist air is cooled to its saturation point, also called the dew point, the air can no longer hold all the moisture and will begin to condense or form water droplets, which is the source of the fog we observe. The saturated air hangs around the coast through the early morning hours of the next day, and, as the air gradually heats up, the fog usually begins to dissipate by midday. A similar process occurs on a warm day when you put a glass of ice water or a cold drink on a table. As the warm air near the cold glass is cooled, it can hold less moisture, so it condenses and starts to drip down the glass.

Coastal fog brings critical moisture, in the otherwise dry summer months, to coastal plant communities, and also serves as an air conditioner for our coastal cities and residents, usually keeping temperatures along the coast pleasant, while the state's inland valleys are scorching.

The Changing Level of the Ocean

The water level along the shoreline changes throughout the day as the tides go in and out, and anyone living along the California coast, or who visits it regularly, quickly notices this. These daily fluctuations are well understood and are very predictable. You can pick up a tide table at a surf shop or sporting goods store that will list the daily high and low tides for the entire year in advance. In addition to these obvious daily variations, there are also longer-term fluctuations in the level of the ocean that take place over weeks, months, or hundreds and thousands of years. The forces that drive the shorter-term changes in sea level are varied, as are those that affect long-term sea level. The magnitude or the amount of these short and long-term changes is different, as are the rates of change. While the differences in water levels between low and high tides along the coast of California may be eight to 10 feet, long-term sea level changes may reach hundreds of feet. They each impact the shoreline in different ways. One of the big challenges we face today as a coastal state, and as a nation, is accurately predicting the sea levels of the future. Rising sea level is creating significant problems for the 100 million people around the world today who live within three feet of sea level. Just how high the level of the ocean will rise in the decades ahead is uncertain. What we do know for sure is that sea level has been rising for about 18,000 years and it will continue to rise for the foreseeable future. This is due to both the natural processes of global warming and also the addition of greenhouse gases into the atmosphere by a lot of different human activities. The continued warming has led to the melting of ice caps and glaciers, and also led to the thermal expansion of seawater as it slowly warms. How high and fast sea level will ultimately are the questions we need to answer.

The Tides: You Cannot Escape Gravity

Because the waters of the ocean move freely, they are affected by the gravitational attraction of both the sun and the moon. Over 300 years ago, Isaac Newton discovered that the moon and the sun exert a gravitational pull on Earth, and that this attraction pulls or distorts the oceans on a regular basis as the relative positions of Earth, the moon, and the sun constantly change. The sun and moon provide the major forces that influence the short-term level of the ocean at any particular time during the day. Newton discovered that the amount of pull that any one body exerts on another is directly proportional to their masses and inversely proportional to the square of the distance between them. The sun is about 27 million times more massive than the moon, but it is about 387 times farther away from Earth. As a result, the moon exerts about twice as much influence on the tides as the sun. Because we know the orbits of the moon and sun quite well, we can predict the level of the tides many years in advance.

The coast of California experiences two high and two low tides each day, with successive highs or lows having different elevations, which we call a mixed semi-diurnal tide (Figure 54). A complete tidal cycle (two highs and two lows) takes place every 24 hours and 50 minutes, so that the highs and lows arrive 50 minutes later each day. When the sun, the moon, and Earth are all aligned, their combined gravitational forces are greatest and produce the largest ranges between low and high tides, known as spring tides (Figure 55). This alignment occurs twice each month at the times of full moon and new moon, and it is at these times of the month that we observe the highest high tides and the lowest low tides. In contrast, when the sun and moon are at right angles to Earth, their gravitational pulls are in partial opposition, and we have lower tidal ranges known as neap tides (Figure 55).

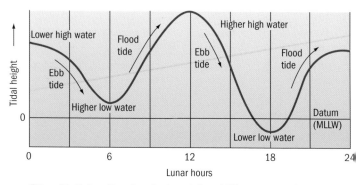

Figure 54. Daily pattern for mixed semi-diurnal tide, as occurs along the California coast.

Tidal heights, as listed in tide tables, are referenced to the mean or average of the lower of the two low tides each day (designated as mean lower low water or MLLW). In Monterey, for example, the highest tide ever recorded was 7.88 feet above MLLW and the lowest was 2.37 feet below

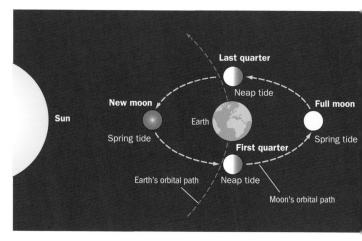

Figure 55. Spring and neap tides, showing the relationship between the Earth, moon, and sun at those times.

MLLW, for a maximum elevation difference of 10.25 feet. Two other extremes are: 11.22 feet between maximum highs and lows at San Diego and 14.08 feet at Crescent City. Tidal ranges vary geographically, however, with some mid-ocean islands experiencing only a foot or two of difference between high and low tides, while the Gulf of California experiences a maximum range of nearly 30 feet between the highest and lowest tides. The Bay of Fundy in Nova Scotia, because of its configuration and location, experiences what has generally been regarded as the greatest tidal range on Earth, about 55 feet between extreme high and low tides. Tidal ranges present significant planning and management issues for California's ports, which are among the most important in the nation due to the volume they handle.

Short-Term Sea Level Changes: Never Turn Your Back on the Ocean

In addition to the gravitational attraction of the sun and moon, strong winds, atmospheric pressure differences, water temperature, and surface currents affect the surface elevation of the ocean. Thus, although tide tables provide an accurate picture of the timing and magnitude of high and low tides expected for each day, at any particular time the local sea level may be affected by other factors. Most changes produced by these other forces are quite small, a few inches perhaps, but they can be greater. On January 27, 1983, for example, owing to warming of the ocean and also to atmospheric pressure differences during the largest El Niño event in many decades, sea levels were the highest ever recorded at tide gauges in San Diego, Los Angeles, and San Francisco. The recorded sea levels in San Diego and Los Angeles were about a foot above those predicted by tide tables. In San Francisco, the recorded high tide was 21 inches above the predicted level, the highest in more than 130 years of record keeping.

A large El Niño affects the elevation of the ocean in two ways. The first is through the pulse or slow moving wave of warm water that moves north from the equatorial region along the coast of North America during one of these events. This forms a low but detectable bulge in the sea surface. The second effect is the response of coastal waters to El Niño weather patterns, especially atmospheric pressure and winds. The seasonally low atmospheric pressure along the coast and the prevailing winds from the west and southwest essentially pile water up along the shoreline. The elevated sea levels along the coastline may extend from Mexico to Canada and persist for several months. The overall effects of elevated sea levels combined with large storm waves is increased inundation and wave impact on low-lying buildings and infrastructure. On a flat or relatively low-sloping beach, an additional foot of sea level may move the high tide 50 feet further landward so waves break closer to the developed shoreline or against the structures themselves.

Global Climate Change and Long-Term Sea Level Fluctuations

During the last Ice Age, huge glaciers covered the mid-continent of the United States and extended down over the area now occupied by the Great Lakes, across what is now Minnesota, Illinois, and Indiana and all the way into Kansas and Nebraska. The Puget Sound area of Washington was scoured out and the area where Seattle now sits was buried under hundreds of feet of ice. A land bridge across the Bering Straits connected Siberia to Alaska, and you could have walked from England to France across the exposed floor of the English Channel. Saber-toothed tigers and lions, dire wolves and giant ground sloths, mammoths and camels all populated California and were preserved in the La Brea tar pits. But the first humans hadn't yet arrived.

Sea level rise is perhaps the most obvious consequence of climate change to residents of coastal California. If we lived in the Central Valley, rising temperatures and reduced rainfall would probably be the issues of greatest concern. If we were in the ski industry, a significant decline in the amount of snowfall in the Sierra Nevada could have devastating effects. Although there have been many editorials, articles, conferences, and debates on global warming, greenhouse gases, and the impacts of human activity on global temperatures, there is no debate or disagreement that Earth and its oceans and atmosphere have been warming for the past 18,000 years. This is not a new phenomenon; the history of Earth has been one of constant climate change (Figure 56).

The climate and temperature of Earth are influenced to a large degree by the amount of heat we get from the sun, which is directly related to how far away we are at any one time. It was recognized nearly 150 years ago that the distance between Earth and the sun changes over time because of irregularities in Earth's orbit, as well as the tilt and wobble of Earth on its axis. As Earth tilts slightly or moves farther away from the sun it receives less solar energy, and as a result, Earth and its atmosphere and oceans cool slightly. When Earth is closer to the sun, global temperatures increase

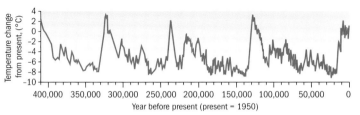

Figure 56. Global temperature variations over the past 400,000 years from present temperature, degrees C.

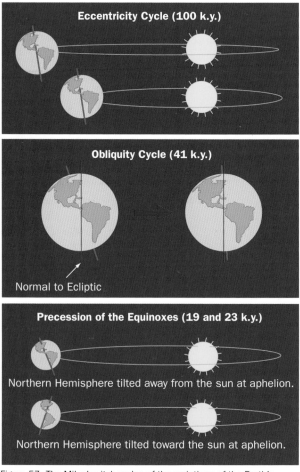

Figure 57. The Milankovitch cycles of the variations of the Earth's wobble (precession), tilt on its axis (obliquity), and eccentricity of its orbit around the sun.

(Figure 57). There are well-understood cycles in these orbital oscillations that span tens of thousands of years and are associated with well-documented warming and cooling intervals that have profoundly affected Earth's surface, its ocean basins, and its life throughout geologic time. These differences in distance are not huge, but they are large enough to lower the temperature of the atmosphere by about 9 degrees F (6 degrees C), which has a profound impact on the distribution of plants and animals, on climate, and on ocean water temperatures.

During cooler periods, the water evaporates from the oceans and accumulates as ice caps and glaciers on Antarctica, Greenland, and other high-latitude areas. This removal of water from the oceans leads to a corresponding global drop in sea level. The amount of sea level drop is related to how cool the climate gets and, therefore, how much ice accumulates on the continents. In addition to the actual removal of seawater, the cooling of the ocean during an Ice Age also has an effect: cold water is denser so it takes up less volume. A drop in temperature of 1.8 degrees F in the surface waters of the ocean will lower sea level by about 6.6 feet, and we believe the surface waters were about 9 degrees F cooler, which by itself would have reduced sea level about 33 feet.

During the last glacial maximum, or cool period, the level of the oceans dropped globally about 350 to 400 feet, and the shoreline moved out to the edge of the continental shelf that surrounds each continent. When Earth gradually moved closer to the sun again and the climate began to warm, the glaciers and ice caps melted and sea level began to rise. This rise was relatively rapid from 18,000 years ago to 7,000 to 8,000 years ago, with an average rate of nearly half an inch per year or about four feet per century. Sea level rise then slowed considerably, and for the last several thousand years or so, the rate of rise has been a little less than a tenth of an inch (two mm) per year (Figure 58).

Rising sea levels are driven by both the melting of ice caps and glaciers and also from the thermal expansion of seawater. All other things being equal, the warmer it gets, the more ice will melt and the higher sea level will rise. There is only so much ice on the surface of Earth, however, so there is a limit to how high sea level can actually rise from climate change.

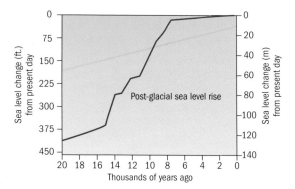

Figure 58. Global sea level rise curve for past 20,000 years.

The mountain glaciers such as those in Glacier National Park and parts of Alaska are relatively small in area, and if they were to continue to retreat and completely melt they would add only about two feet to the total level of the oceans. Greenland is a different story, however, and if its ice cover were to completely melt or break up and become ice bergs, sea level would rise about 24 feet! Greenland is melting at an increasing rate, however, and 24 feet of sea-level rise would inundate some large cities situated at sea level: London, New Orleans, Miami, and much of the San Francisco Bay area, to name a few. Antarctica has by far the largest volume of ice, enough to raise sea level globally by about 200 feet were it all to melt. The ice shelves surrounding parts of Antarctica are melting at rates that are historically unprecedented, but the largest volume of ice in Antarctica lies in the interior of the continent, locked in by mountains, so it is not all going to melt anytime soon. While there is much more water locked up in Greenland and Antarctica than in the world's other mountain glaciers and icecaps, measurements over the past decade indicate that these latter sources have contributed about 60 percent of the meltwater that has been flowing into the oceans, while Greenland's melting ice sheets have contributed only 28 percent, and the Antarctic ice sheet another 12 percent.

A second factor influencing sea level was mentioned above, the thermal expansion of seawater. As water gets warmer, it expands and takes up more volume. Your 50-gallon home water heater was built to accommodate thermal expansion. Fifty gallons of water at 40 degrees F will expand to about 51 gallons when heated to 140 degrees. The upper several hundred meters of the ocean is warming and the resulting expansion of all that water is estimated to account for somewhere between one-fourth and one-third of the observed sea-level rise over the past several thousand years, or about 6.6 feet for each degree C the surface oceans have warmed.

Several other factors determine how this gradual sea level rise will affect any particular coastal area. One important consideration is whether the adjacent landmass is rising, stable, or subsiding. Although sea level rises and falls globally depending mostly upon the total volume of water in the oceans at any given time, the vertical movement of the land can compound or counteract the rise in sea level. Long Beach, New Orleans, and Venice, Italy, for example, are all areas that have undergone many feet of subsidence over the past century. The land in these and other coastal locations around the world is sinking as a result of the loading of Earth's crust by the deposition of thousands of feet of sediments (deposited on the delta of the Mississippi River, for example, in the case of New Orleans), or from groundwater or oil withdrawal (Long Beach) from the subsurface. Consequently, the relative rate of sea level rise in New Orleans and Venice as recorded on tide gauges is much greater than the global rate because we are measuring the combined effects of the land sinking and sea level rising.

The sea level at Grand Isle, Louisiana, near New Orleans, has been rising at 9.24 millimeters per year over the past

60 years, equivalent to a little over three feet per century (Figure 59A). Juneau, Alaska, in contrast, is actually rising as a result of a slow rebound of the land from the removal of thousands of feet of glacial ice that covered and depressed it 20,000 years ago. The rebound or uplift rate of the land surface is faster than the rate of sea-level rise. The tide gauge

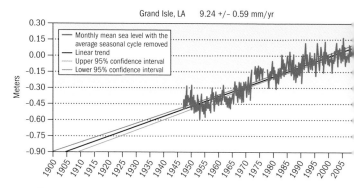

Figure 59A. Tide gage record showing sea level changes relative to the land at Grand Isle, Louisiana, for the past 60 years. (from http://tidesandcurrents.noaa.gov/sltrends/sltrends.shtml)

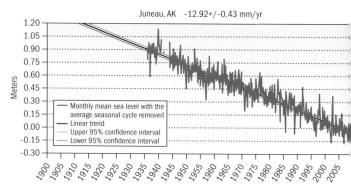

Figure 59B. Tide gage record showing sea level changes relative to the land at Juneau, Alaska, for the past 70 years. (from http://tidesandcurrents.noaa.gov/sltrends/sltrends.shtml)

at Juneau actually shows a drop in sea level relative to land of nearly 13 millimeters per year over the past 70 years, equivalent to 4.24 feet per 100 years (Figure 59B)! Sea-level rise, especially when combined with hurricanes, is a major concern for the residents of New Orleans. In Juneau, there may be other concerns related to climate change, but sea-level rise is not one of them.

How do we fare along the coast of California in regard to sea-level rise compared to Juneau and New Orleans, or other states, and what kind of problems can we expect to face in the years ahead? The best indicators of long-term sea-level changes are the records from the tide gauges scattered along the coastlines of each state (Figure 60). Like the gauges from Alaska and Louisiana discussed above, those in California are keeping track of relative sea level, or the rise or fall in sea level relative to that section of coastline where the gauge is located. There are 12 gauges continuously recording sea level along the California coast while we go about our lives

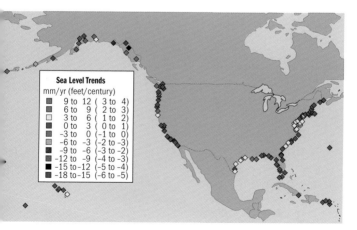

Figure 60. Local sea level rise rates from tide gage stations around the coastlines of the United States. (from http://tidesandcurrents.noaa .gov/sltrends/sltrends.shtml)

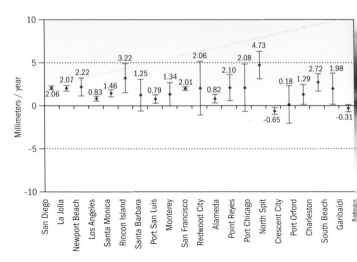

Figure 61. Local sea level rise rates along the west coast of the United States. (from http://tidesandcurrents.noaa.gov/sltrends/sltrends.shtml)

worrying about other things. The longest record is from San Francisco and it extends back to 1855. With the exception of Humboldt County, along the far-north coast, however, all California's tidal stations indicate average local sea-level rise rates of between 0.79 and 2.22 millimeters per year, or 3.2 to 8.8 inches per 100 years (Figure 61). Overall this is a very narrow range, and is somewhat surprising, considering that the coast of California is 1,100 miles long and very active tectonically.

The two tide gauges north of Cape Mendocino, one at Eureka and one at Crescent City, record a very different history, reflecting the unique geologic setting of this stretch of coastline. The relative sea-level rise rate at Eureka is 4.73 millimeters per year, over twice as high as any other place along the California coast. At Crescent City, sea level is actually dropping at 0.65 millimeters per year relative to the land. The entire Pacific Northwest coast from Cape Mendocino to Vancouver Island is adjacent to the

Cascadia Subduction Zone (Figure 62), where the offshore Juan de Fuca plate is colliding with and descending beneath the North-American plate. This has pulled down the coastline in some areas, Eureka for example, where sea level shows a much higher rate of rise than other areas further south. The plate collision process has produced uplift in other locations, Crescent City for example, which is why the tide gauge shows sea level dropping relative to the coastline. One of the serious hazards of living along the coast near a subduction

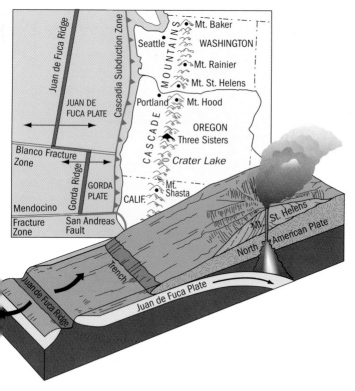

Figure 62. Map view and cross section of the Cascadia Subduction Zone, which extends from Cape Mendocino to Vancouver Island.

zone is the tsunamis that are periodically generated by large earthquakes just offshore. You will have to wait until the next chapter to read more about tsunamis and other hazards of living directly on the coastline.

Two other important factors affecting sea-level rise and its impact on any particular coastal area are the elevation and the topography of the shoreline. Along low-lying, nearly-flat coastal areas such as North Carolina, Florida, Louisiana, or even around the edges of San Francisco Bay, a three-foot rise in sea level may advance the shoreline landward several thousand feet. When the Cape Hatteras Lighthouse was built in 1870, it was 1,500 feet from the shoreline. Sixty-five years later, a gradually rising sea level had moved high tide to within 125 feet of the structure. In 1999, after lots of debate, the National Park Service spent $15.5 million (in 2008 dollars) to pick up the 4,800-ton lighthouse and move it 2,900 feet inland, not a simple undertaking. The consequences of a continued rise in sea level along much of the Atlantic and Gulf coasts are very serious, the impacts are going to increase and decisions will need to be made. In places like Bangladesh, where millions of people live on fertile but very low-lying deltaic land, a rise in sea level of a few feet, which typically happens during a cyclone or typhoon, can inundate huge areas with large losses of life. The disastrous tsunami in the northern Indian Ocean that took place in December 2004 was a deadly reminder of the risks of living close to sea level.

Low bluffs or cliffs back 72 percent of the coastline of California, so a few feet of sea-level rise in these areas will not be disastrous. For the other 28 percent—much of the coastline of Los Angeles County, and parts of Ventura, Orange and San Diego counties—where the shoreline is quite flat and where intensive development has taken place at or close to beach level, a three-foot rise in sea level will have very significant effects (Figure 63). Similarly, the levees protecting much of the Sacramento-San Joaquin

Figure 63. Street sign in beachfront development along the Malibu coast. Photo Gary Griggs.

delta area would probably fail with three feet of sea-level rise.

San Francisco's Bay Conservation and Development Commission (or BCDC), an intergovernmental agency that plans for and has permit authority for how land is used around the shoreline of San Francisco Bay, carried out a study in 2005 to determine how a sea-level rise of 40-cm to 1.40-meters would affect the development around the bay. This is the most recent range in the projected sea level rise for the year 2100. The results of this analysis shocked most people who have seen them and don't bode well for the future. Much of shallow, marshy area around the margins of San Francisco Bay has been filled over the past 150 years for a variety of uses, including housing, freeways, airports, and stadiums. Because transporting and placing engineered fill is expensive, there was no reason at the time to add more fill than was necessary to get the ground level just above the highest tides. But as sea-level rise has progressed, it has become clear that much of this development would be submerged by a meter of sea-level rise (Figure 64). The nearly complete inundation of the San Francisco and Oakland international airports is perhaps the most disruptive potential

0 0.5 1   2 Miles ↑

bcdc San Francisco Bay
Conservation and Development Commission

Area vulnerable to an approximate 16 inch sea level rise
Area vulnerable to an approximate 55 inch sea level rise

Figure 64. Areas that would be inundated by a 40-cm (16-in) and a
1.4-meter (55-in) rise in sea level in the southern portion of the San
Francisco Bay area (Map courtesy of San Francisco Bay Conservation
and Development Commission).

impact (Figures 65 and 66). In December 2008, Gover-
nor Schwarzenegger issued an Executive Order requesting
that all state agencies develop plans for both mitigating
the effects of climate change and adapting to the expected
changes. There are some serious and expensive challenges to
adapting all the low-lying development around the margins
of San Francisco Bay to a meter or more of sea-level rise. We

bcdc San Francisco Bay
Conservation and Development Commission

☐ Area vulnerable to an approximate 16 inch sea level rise
■ Area vulnerable to an approximate 55 inch sea level rise

Figure 65. Areas that would be inundated by a 40-cm (16-in) and a 1.4-meter (55-in) rise in sea level in the San Francisco International Airport area (Map courtesy of San Francisco Conservation and Development Commission).

still have some time, but we need to begin to think through our options carefully.

For the exposed outer California coast, it is not just the rise in sea level but also the waves that break closer to the shoreline that will impact coastal development and will gradually lead to increased inundation, damage, and destruction. Coastal residents have built thousands of

San Francisco Bay
Conservation and Development Commission

0 0.5 1   2 Miles ↑

   Area vulnerable to an approximate 16 inch sea level rise
   Area vulnerable to an approximate 55 inch sea level rise

Figure 66. Areas that would be inundated by a 40-cm (16-in) and a 1.4-meter (55-in) rise in sea level in the east San Francisco Bay area (Map courtesy of San Francisco Bay Conservation and Development Commission).

homes directly on the shoreline, in some cases cantilevered out over the beach (Figure 67). We need to realize and accept that the present position of the shoreline or sea cliff is a temporary one, and simply a reflection of where sea level is today. The questions we need to begin to answer are: How much higher will sea level rise? How soon is it likely that we will reach this level? And how do we adapt to this impending change?

Figure 67. Houses in Malibu cantilevered out over the shoreline. Photo Kenneth and Gabrielle Adelman, California Coastal Records Project, www.CaliforniaCoastline.org.

Global Warming and Future Predictions: What Can We Expect Next?

Over the past decade or so, the discussion of climate change and global warming has gone from the University seminar room to city council chambers and the halls of Congress. For many, it seemed inconceivable that anything humans could do would actually have any significant effect on atmosphere and global temperatures. Many of these same people also believed that the oceans were infinite and that our fishing industry could never make a dent in the fish populations. With 90 percent of the large oceanic or pelagic fish like swordfish and blue-fin tuna now gone, it is clear that billions of human beings can have impacts on global scales.

We know that human activity since the Industrial Revolution began in the late 1800s has significantly increased the concentration of carbon dioxide and other gases (methane, nitrous oxide, and chlorofluorocarbons, for example) in the atmosphere. These greenhouse gases allow shortwave radiation from the sun to pass through the atmosphere and warm Earth. Like the glass in a greenhouse or the windows in the family minivan, these greenhouse gases don't allow the heat that is given off by Earth as long-wave back radiation to escape back into the atmosphere. Just as your car heats up on a sunny day when the windows are rolled up, Earth's oceans and atmosphere have been gradually warming as we have rolled up the windows in the atmosphere. Greenhouse gases have built up from a combination of fossil fuel combustion, the burning of tropical rain forests, and other industrial and agricultural processes that produce nitrous oxide, methane, and chlorofluorocarbons. The atmospheric concentration of carbon dioxide, the most abundant gas, has gone from about 272 parts per million (ppm) in 1870, at the beginning of the Industrial

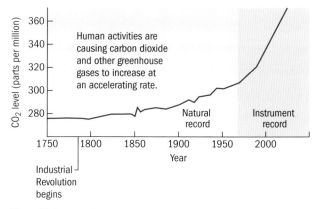

Figure 68. Increase in carbon dioxide content in the atmosphere since 1750.

Revolution, to 387 ppm in 2008, an increase of 42 percent (Figure 68). This is a huge increase.

Separating out the effects of greenhouse gases from the ongoing natural cycle of global warming is a difficult problem, and many different studies have attempted to sort out these influences. When all the natural factors that affect the climate are fed into a computer model, the resulting graph does not match the temperatures that have been measured. The global warming since 1960 can only be explained if both natural processes and human-produced greenhouse gases are taken into account. The 2007 report by the Intergovernmental Panel on Climate Change (IPCC), which is an international group of hundreds of scientists, states with 90 percent certainty that human activity is largely responsible for the increased global warming we are now experiencing. There are few things that scientists will agree on with a 90 percent confidence. This is one we ought to pay attention to.

Global warming is a certainty and the scientific consensus is that our greenhouse gas emissions are contributing significantly to this process. We also know precisely how fast sea level has been rising at different locations along the state's coastline in response to this warming. Satellite measurements of global sea surface elevations over the past 15 years indicate an 83 percent increase in the rate of rise from an average rate of 1.8 millimeters per year between 1950 and 2000 (Figure 69) to about 3.3 millimeters per year. While it is difficult to know how this will impact the California coast, sea level will continue to rise for at least the next several hundred years as a result of the greenhouse gases we have already emitted. What we don't know yet is how much faster it may rise and how high it will eventually reach. This will depend primarily upon how much of Greenland and Antarctic ice melt and how much the surface waters of the ocean warm.

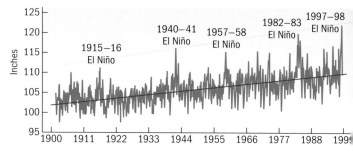

Figure 69. Tide gage record showing sea level changes relative to land at Fort Point in San Francisco. (from http://tidesandcurrents.noaa.gov/sltrends/sltrends.shtml)

The 2007 IPCC report projects a sea-level rise between seven and 19 inches by 2100. Many scientists believe that because of the international nature of the IPCC, and the economic interest of different countries, that these estimates are very conservative. The values are based simply on different graphical extensions or extrapolations from the past century of data, however, and don't include the recent satellite data showing an increased rate of sea-level rise. They also don't include any of the recently documented rapid reduction of the ice cover in the Arctic Ocean, the breakup of Greenland's ice cover or the breaking off of the ice shelves of Antarctica. For these reasons, many scientists believe that a three-foot rise in sea level by 2100 is a reasonable expectation to plan for. We can hope for the best, but we should be planning for the worst.

The Ocean in Motion

Waves and beaches are inextricably connected, tied at the hip, so to speak. Without waves we would have no beaches. They are the single most important process affecting the beaches and coastline of California every day. There is no question that the underlying geology and tectonic setting has produced the large-scale landforms, such as the mountains, the cliffs, and the terraces, but that's long-term. It is the waves that impact and shape and reshape the coastline and beaches day in and day out, winter and spring, summer and fall.

There are many different kinds of waves out there in the ocean, some we can see, and others we cannot. The tides that slosh back and forth from one side of the Pacific Ocean to the other twice a day in response to the gravitational pull of the moon and the sun are one kind of very long wave. Large disruptions or displacements of the seafloor, by undersea earthquakes, volcanic eruptions, or landslides, generate another type of very fast moving wave, which we recognize as tsunamis or seismic sea waves. We have now recognized internal waves that move beneath the surface of the ocean along density interfaces. Internal waves could be observed in a small aquarium if we filled it with different colored fluids of slightly different densities and we disturbed or shook the aquarium and vibrated the different layers.

The Endless Summer: Wind and Waves

The waves we see breaking on the shoreline, those most visible to us and the ones that make surfing possible, are generated by the wind. No matter where we are along the California coast, there are waves breaking on the beach arriving from somewhere; they might have been generated by the afternoon wind a few miles offshore, or may have traveled thousands of miles from a storm off of New Zealand many days earlier. All we need to begin to make waves in the ocean is some wind. Just like you can create small ripples or waves in your cup of coffee or tea as you blow to cool it down, the wind accomplishes the same thing on a much larger scale on the ocean surface.

When the wind first begins to blow across the sea surface, the friction of the air moving across the water will create small ripples. Once a ripple has formed, there is now a steeper side against which the wind can exert more pressure. This allows the energy of the wind to be more effectively transmitted to the water surface and the ripples can begin to grow into small waves. As long as the wind continues to blow, more energy can be transferred to the sea surface and the waves can increase in size. Because the wind doesn't blow at a completely uniform velocity and because the sea surface is rarely smooth, the pattern of waves initially created will be somewhat irregular and choppy. If we were at sea in a ship during a storm we would see small and large waves, some forming as we watched and others that were passing by the ship, having been formed miles away by some other storm. This irregular mixture of waves of different heights and lengths is referred to by oceanographers as *sea*.

If the wind keeps blowing in the same general direction long enough the waves will begin to travel in that direction and sort themselves out. As the waves increase in size, having been given more energy by the wind, we can begin to recognize them as individual features with some recognizable properties. Each wave has a *crest* and a *trough*, and can be defined with a *height*, a *wavelength*, a *period* and a *velocity*, or speed (Figure 70). When the waves leaving a storm area have sorted themselves out and are more uniformly shaped, we refer to this condition as *swell*. You will often hear on the weather channel, or when coastal wave conditions are being described, that there is a "six-foot *swell* at

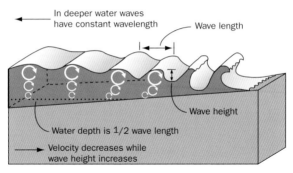

In deeper water waves have constant wavelength

Wave length

Wave height

Water depth is 1/2 wave length

Velocity decreases while wave height increases

Figure 70. A group of waves will have a distinct wave length (distance between two successive crests), wave period (time in seconds for two successive crest to pass a point), and wave height (vertical distance between the trough and the crest).

11 seconds and a local two-foot sea." The swell has come from much farther away and is more uniform, while the sea is generated by the local winds and is usually more irregular and much smaller.

Wave period is expressed in seconds and is simply the time it takes for two successive wave crests to pass a single point. If you are standing on a pier, for example, you can look down and watch the waves passing beneath you. If you looked at your watch and counted how many seconds it took for two wave crests to pass the same piling, you would have measured the wave period. Most of the waves we see breaking along our coast are commonly in the five to 10 or 12 second range. There are many locally generated waves that have shorter periods, and occasionally we will see waves along the California coast that have traveled thousands of miles that have periods of 15 seconds or longer.

Wavelength is just the distance between two successive crests and usually listed in feet or meters. If you throw a stone into a pond or lake you will create a set of waves that move out in a circular pattern from where the stone hit the

Figure 71. Waves with long wavelengths approaching the shoreline at Pleasure Point in Santa Cruz. Photo Gary Griggs.

water and they will have wavelengths we can measure in inches. Waves far out at sea or even those that approach the shoreline will usually have wavelengths of hundreds of feet (Figure 71).

The height of a wave is just the vertical distance, usually given in feet, from the crest or highest point on the wave to the trough or lowest point. Ripples or very small waves a few inches in height form in a lake or pond, but surfers don't usually begin to get excited or interested until the waves get up to five or six feet or more. But how high can they get? Wave height and how we measure it is often a source of some serious arguments among surfers, and at stake recently has been the $50,000 annual prize for riding the biggest wave in any particular year. Scripps Institution of Oceanography, working with the state Department of Boating and Waterways and the U.S. Army Corps of Engineers maintains a system of 21 wave recorders along the California coast. These are either surface buoys which are anchored in deep water some distance offshore, or bottom mounted instruments closer to shore that accurately measure wave height as well as wave period and direction of travel. This information is all available online to erase all doubts about how high the waves actually were that afternoon (http://cdip.ucsd.edu/).

As the wind continues to blow during an offshore storm, the waves will gradually increase in height. It is the combination of the wind speed, the length of time the wind blows, as well as the distance over which it blows (which is called the *fetch*), that ultimately determine how large the waves can get. Through a combination of observations, measurements, and an understanding of how energy from the wind is transmitted to the sea surface, oceanographers who study waves have developed relationships between the wind conditions and the size of waves that can be formed (Table 2). What has been discovered over years of studying waves is that in deep, offshore water the speed at which the waves travel is dependent on their wavelengths or their periods. The wavelength (L), if we are measuring in feet, is equal to 5.12 times the period (T) squared, or $L = 5.12 \ T^2$. Thus a wave with a period of five

TABLE 2 Conditions necessary to produce a fully developed sea at different wind speeds and the characteristics of the resulting waves

Wind speed in miles/hr	Fetch in miles	Duration in hours	Average wave height in ft	Average wave length in ft	Average period in seconds	Highest 10% of waves in ft
12	15	2.8	1	35	3.2	2.5
19	48	7	2.9	73	4.6	6.9
25	109	11.5	5.9	130	6.2	12.8
31	236	18.5	10.5	203	7.7	22.3
37	409	27.5	16.7	293	9.1	34.4
43	678	37.5	24.3	398	10.8	50.2
50	1,043	50	33.8	520	12.4	70.2
56	1,517	65.2	45.6	661	13.9	93.2

seconds has a wavelength of 5.12×5^2 or about 128 feet. The velocity (V) or speed of the waves is also easy to calculate with V = 5.12T, so the same five second wave has a velocity of 5.12×5 or 25.6 feet per second, which is 17.5 miles per hour, faster than most of us can run. A 10 second wave, or a wave with a period of 10 seconds between each crest, is moving twice as fast or about 35 miles per hour at sea. The longest swell ever recorded had a period of 22.5 seconds and came out of the South Atlantic and measured along the Dover coast of England. Using the formulas above, these waves would have had a wavelength of half a mile and a velocity of 78 miles an hour!

Because the speed of a wave is directly related to its length or period, the longer waves will move out away from the shorter ones during a storm simply because they are traveling faster. These longer waves may often be traveling faster than the storm front that created them and can arrive at the beach and create great surfing conditions some time before the wind and rain actually reach the coast (Figure 72).

While we say that the waves move or travel at a certain velocity, it is actually the form of the wave and not the water itself

Figure 72. Surfing a large wave. Photo Schmuel Thaler, *Santa Cruz Sentinel*.

that advances across the sea surface. If we watched some object floating in the water, or if you are out in the waves yourself, you will notice that as each wave passes by, you or the object you are watching will rise and sink and follow a circular orbit or path, returning to nearly the same place you started (Figure 73).

Figure 73. As a wave passes, the water particles move in a circular motion. While the wave form advances, the water particles return to approximately their original position.

The individual particles of water are following the same orbits and it is only the waveform that is advancing across the ocean surface. We can observe the same process by tying a rope to a post and moving the rope up and down to make waves in the rope. The rope itself doesn't advance towards the post; it is just the waveform we have created that is moving. The wave that people create by raising their arms inside a sports stadium is exactly the same process. The people aren't moving around the stadium, only the form of the wave is.

Rogue or Giant Waves

The German container carrier *MS München* left Bremerhaven, Germany, on a cold day in late 1978 headed for Savannah, Georgia. On December 12, the ship, two-and-a-half football fields long and described as unsinkable, vanished with one unintelligible distress call. All that was found in a wide search of the general area was some scattered debris and an unlaunched lifeboat that was originally secured on the deck 65 feet above the water line. Its attachment pins had been "twisted as though hit by an extreme force." The best guess was that the ship had been struck by a very large wave.

While seaman for many years have described huge waves or walls of water at sea, they were not usually given much credence until recently. Encounters with such large waves have become more frequent over the past 15 years or so, indicating that perhaps these were not all just sailors' exaggerations or nightmares. In February 1995, the *Queen Elizabeth II* encountered what was described as a 90-foot wall of water in the North Atlantic. Two cruise ships that take tourists across the South Atlantic to Antarctica, the *Bremen* and the *Caledonian Star*, collided with rogue waves nearly 100-feet high within a week of each other in early 2001. Both vessels had their bridge windows broken and the Bremen drifted without navigation or propulsion for two hours. The First

Officer of the *Caledonian Star* stated that it was "*just like a mountain, a wall of water coming against us.*" In March 2007, Holland America's cruise ship *MS Prinsendam* was hit by a 70-foot-high wave in the Antarctic part of a voyage around the tip of South America. In the 21 years between 1981 and 2001, 124 ships over 600 feet long were reported to have sunk, often by what is usually called "severe weather."

A five-year project was initiated by the European Space Agency in 2000 to look into how common rogue waves might be and if they might explain the losses of these large ships. Using twin satellites that use radar to observe waves at the sea surface, scientists initially evaluated 30,000 images for a three-week period when the *Bremen* and the *Caledonian Star* were damaged. Even though this was a brief period of time, the team of scientists identified 10 individual giant waves from around the world oceans that were over 80 feet in height! This came as a big surprise and provided strong evidence that large rogue waves are far more common that was previously believed. This initial series of observations also revealed that these giant waves often occur where ordinary wind waves encounter ocean currents. The strength of the current seems to concentrate the wave energy, much like a lens will concentrate light. These conditions take place far out to sea, however, so no need to worry about rogue waves attacking you on the beach. Although, as will be discussed later in this chapter, bottom conditions near the coast can cause very large waves to form and break, providing some challenging and exciting conditions for some surfers.

The End of a Long Journey: Waves Meet the Shoreline

Some waves formed during storms far out to sea in the Pacific Ocean will ultimately head towards California where they will leave deep water behind, cross the shallow continental shelf, and begin to approach the shoreline. Depending upon the wavelength of the particular waves, they will begin to impinge on or feel the bottom somewhere on the shelf. Along the coast of California the shelf ranges in width from less than a mile off of Big Sur to over 25 miles off San Francisco.

As a wave passes through the ocean, it not only displaces the water at the surface but also moves the water at depth. This is why when you are diving under the waves or scuba diving in shallow water, you will feel the water moving back and forth at depth. The depth at which water is set in motion by the waves passing overhead is equal to one-half of their wavelength. So to keep it simple, if the waves passing by at the surface have a wavelength of 200 feet, the circular motion involved with the passage of each wave-form will extend to a depth of half of this or about 100 feet (Figure 74).

As soon as this deeper portion of wave begins to feel the bottom, it will begin to slow down due to friction with the seafloor, while the portion that we see at the sea surface continues to travel at its original speed. Several wave

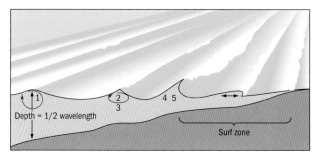

Figure 74. Waves undergo changes as they approach the shoreline. The height increases while the wavelength and speed decrease, however, the wave period remains unchanged. A wave will break when the ratio of wave height to water depth is about 3:4.

properties now begin to change because of this bottom friction. Due to the drag on the bottom as the wave continues towards shallower water, the overall wave velocity will begin to slow and the wavelength will begin to shorten as well. Because the circular or orbital motion of the water particles beneath the wave is being compressed or confined into shallower and shallower depths, the crest of the wave at the sea surface will begin to increase in height. While the waveform in the open ocean is a long series of broad swells and troughs, in shallow water this will change to a series of steeper and more distinct wave crests separated by flatter troughs. Eventually the portion of the wave above the sea surface will become steep and unstable. When the ratio of the wave height to the water depth is about 3:4, the wave will finally break. Thus a three-foot-high wave will break in about four feet of water, and a six-foot-high wave will break in about eight feet of water.

Waves can transmit enormous amounts of energy, and they are continuously being created while the wind is blowing, sort of an endless summer for wave formation. Thus, they are renewable, which is one reason why engineers and oceanographers have labored for years on schemes to utilize wave energy. To provide some sense of the power involved in waves, anyone who has seen storm waves batter a cliff, pier, or other oceanfront structure has witnessed the tremendous power they expend (Figure 75). A 10-foot wave can exert over 1,000 pounds of pressure per square foot, and wave pressures over 12,000 pounds or six tons per square foot have been recorded.

During a huge storm in 1914, wave run-up extinguished the Trinidad Head Light at an elevation of nearly 200 feet above sea level (Figure 21). The St. George Reef lighthouse near Crescent City experienced a massive storm in 1923 in which breaking waves swept over the foundation platform for the lighthouse, which was 70 feet above the water, tearing a large generator from its foundation. Restaurants along

Figure 75. Wave breaking at Lighthouse Point, Santa Cruz. Photo Schmuel Thaler, *Santa Cruz Sentinel*.

Cardiff's restaurant row in northern San Diego County were severely damaged during the January–February 1983 storms when large waves threw cobbles and boulders weighing up to 1,200 pounds into the buildings and onto the highway. These are just a few examples of the power of waves crashing on the coastline, and is one major reason why anything built directly on the shoreline, whether on the cliff, dune, or beach, while providing great satisfaction for six to nine months each year, is in a very vulnerable location every winter.

Wave Energy: Can We Use It?

The waves just offshore contain huge amounts of energy. Technologies for converting wave energy into electrical power are evolving, and renewable energy companies are increasingly interested in converting the energy of

California's ocean waters into electricity. The energy in a wave is proportional to the square of its height. A wave six feet high represents an energy flow of about 25 kilowatts (34 horsepower) for each three feet of wave front, enough to light 250 100-watt light bulbs. We are going to need a lot more energy than this, however, to make a dent in our present non-renewable systems. But can we harness any of this offshore energy?

The development of a renewable ocean energy industry in the United States has been hampered to date by a number of regulatory challenges. The regulatory system was not designed to encourage pilot and demonstration projects and, related to this lack of certainty, there has been a general lack of investment in basic research and the development of new technologies. State and federal governments need to develop permitting processes that encourage development of demonstration projects while being sensitive to protection of the marine environment. If we are to make any progress with wave energy, regulation of ocean power development needs to be clear, efficient, and organized with a single lead agency coupled with common sense.

There are now over 20 companies around the world that are developing wave energy technologies, of which six have now gone commercial. The technologies that are the most advanced for conversion of wave energy into electrical power fall into four general types:

1. An oscillating water column, where the rise and fall of the water in a tube as a wave passes forces air through a turbine that generates electricity.
2. Attenuators, such as the snake-like Pelamis, where an elongate and segmented floating tube, about the length of a submarine, flexes as waves pass by with the up and down motion driving a generator.

3. Overtopping, where waves spill over into a floating reservoir with the return flow of water into the ocean driving a turbine.
4. Wave buoys or point absorbers, where passing waves cause the structure to rise and fall and uses this motion to turn a turbine.

In September of 2007, Portugal completed the installation of the world's first commercial power plant that harnesses wave energy. It uses three articulated steel "sea snakes" (the Pelamis system; Figure 76) three miles off the country's

Figure 76. Pelamis, which uses a series of large, articulated floating tubes, is the only commercial wave power system now in operation and was placed off the coast of Portugal in 2008. It generates 2.25 megawatts of power, enough to supply about 1,500 households. Photo Pelamis Wave.

northern coast. They produce a combined 2.25 megawatts, enough to power about 1,500 homes with electricity, but there is optimism for a 10-fold expansion over the next few years. Now, there are also experimental wave energy plants in Japan, Norway, Britain, Sweden, Russia, and India.

In December 2007, one of California's major power companies signed the nation's first commercial power purchase agreement for wave energy, a modest two-megawatt project that would capture wave energy off the Humboldt coast that expects to begin producing power in 2012.

The potential amount of energy is significant and the technology is developing quickly, but we still have a long ways to go. These efforts need to be encouraged, and we need to streamline the permitting and regulatory process and get some projects in the water. The Electrical Power Research Institute believes that ocean renewable energy in U.S. waters has the potential to provide 10 percent of today's electrical demand. It is still, however, too early to predict with any certainty how important wave energy will be in our future.

Waiting for the Perfect Wave: Wave Interference and Sets

Sitting on a bluff or a beach somewhere watching the waves roll in, or being in the water itself, you will notice, most days, that the waves come in sets, or intervals, when the waves will increase in height and then get smaller again. If you are surfing, you may notice three or four large waves, when everyone attempts to take off, and then you might sit and wait for several minutes or longer for another set. You are observing the everyday process of *wave interference*. Along any stretch of coastline there will usually be more than one group of waves arriving on any particular day, and they are probably coming from different directions, although that might be hard to tell while standing on the beach. Large waves may be arriving from a storm in the north Pacific, while smaller waves are approaching from the tropics, and then there may be a local wind swell from just offshore. As these different waves approach the shoreline, they will begin to interact or interfere with one another. This will produce a series of larger and smaller waves in some pattern that will be different every day depending upon the characteristics of the individual storm or local wind waves that are arriving. When the crests of two different wave groups are in phase and arrive at the same time at the shoreline, they will reinforce one another, or constructively interfere, producing higher than normal wave crests. If the waves are of nearly the same period, perhaps one group of waves being 10 seconds between crests and another being 11 seconds, then there may be a set of four or five waves that will form that are much higher than the others, providing good surfing conditions. The waves will then gradually move out of phase and the crest of one group of waves will arrive at the same time as the trough of the other group, and the waves will tend to cancel each other out as we observe *destructive interference,* with the resulting waves being much smaller or lower for a few minutes. Because the groups of waves that arrive on any beach will be different every day, there is no pattern or reason why the seventh wave or the ninth wave, or any other should be larger. It is a totally random process depending only on where storm waves are coming from, and the characteristics, such as period and height, of the different waves that arrive at any particular period of time.

Refraction: Bending the Waves

Most waves arriving at the shoreline approach the coast at some angle rather than coming from directly offshore. Waves reaching the coast in the winter months along much of the California coast typically originate from storms in the North Pacific and, therefore, approach from the northwest. A south swell, or waves arriving from the Southern Hemisphere, is common during the summer months in southern and central California and may provide excellent surfing conditions at a time when waves are normally considerably smaller. Many of these waves are generated from storms off Antarctica, New Zealand, or Australia and have traveled thousands of miles from their origin.

Think about a wave approaching the beach at an angle to the shoreline. As the water gets shallower near the coast, the portion of the wave closest to the beach "feels" the sea floor first and begins to slow down, while the seaward portion of the wave crest in deeper water continues to travel at its original speed. This results in the bending or *refraction* of the wave fronts as they approach the shoreline

Figure 77. Wave refraction at Paradise Cove, Malibu. Photo Bruce Perry, CSULB Geological Sciences.

(Figure 77). As refraction continues, the wave fronts tend to become roughly parallel to the underwater contours. On an irregular, rocky coastline, refraction causes wave energy to bend around points or headlands or shallow areas on the seafloor, thereby concentrating wave energy and increasing wave heights (Figure 78). The same bending, or refraction, process leads to wave fronts diverging in bays or over deeper areas such as submarine canyons, which leads to lower waves or energy dissipation (Figure 78). A mound on the shallow seafloor can then act like a lens to focus the wave energy and cause the waves to converge or increase in height passing over the mound. The refraction and, therefore, gradual breaking of the waves around a point or headland produces some of the best surfing spots in California, Malibu, Rincon, and Steamer Lane, to name a few (Figure 79). Surfing without wave refraction would produce very short rides.

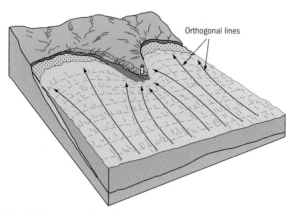

Figure 78. Wave refraction will concentrate energy, producing higher waves at a headland, and disperse wave energy, producing lower waves in a bay.

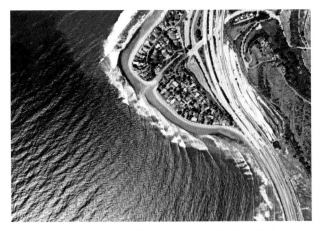

Figure 79. Wave refraction at Rincon Point, one of California's premier surfing areas. Photo California Department of Boating and Waterways.

California's Biggest Waves: What's Up at Mavericks

A new location has been added to the other well-known, legendary California surfing spots within the past decade, Mavericks, just offshore from Pillar Point at Half Moon Bay. While almost unknown, except to a few locals for years, the massive waves that break there each winter have now spawned a big wave surfing contest that draws competitors from all over the world. There are reasons why bigger waves rise out of the water here than anywhere else on the California coast, and new ways of imaging the seafloor have allowed marine and coastal geologists to see the topography that makes this possible.

The geology of the seafloor at Mavericks is unique in several respects (Figure 80). First, the resistant sedimentary rocks exposed on the seafloor stand up as rugged ridges that have been folded into distinct patterns.

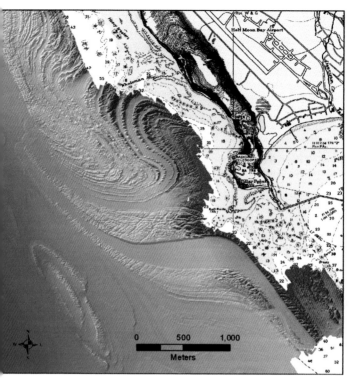

Figure 80. Multibeam bathymetry of the seafloor off Pillar Point showing the folded layers of sedimentary rocks. Mavericks is the rocky area immediately southwest of Pillar Point. Image Sea Floor Mapping Lab CSUMB.

Secondly, the water depth changes very quickly due to the rocks exposed on the seafloor. Bedrock outcrops rise in elevation so that water depths of 75 feet shallows very quickly to about 25 feet, causing the waves to "jack" up or increase quickly in height over a short distance. Finally, the particular outcrop or seafloor exposure where the largest waves form is a mound so that the wave fronts are refracted around this bulge (Figure 81), and wave energy converges

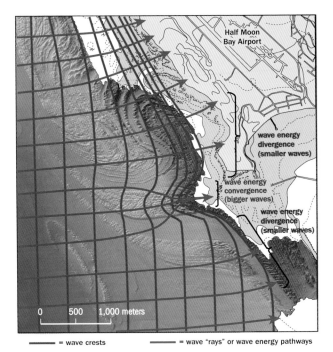

======= = wave crests   ======= = wave "rays" or wave energy pathways

Figure 81. Wave refraction at Mavericks. The blue lines indicate how wave crests approach the coastline and the red lines are wave "rays," or energy pathways, and illustrate how wave energy is dispersed or concentrated. The surfing break at Mavericks is at the large red arrow. Image Sea Floor Mapping Lab CSUMB.

or piles up to create 40- to 50-foot-monster waves under ideal conditions.

There are many areas along the California coast where the local wave climate, or the heights of the waves that break, differ significantly over relatively short distances, which is typically due to wave refraction. During the Prohibition era in late April 1930, large swells damaged the tip of the Long Beach breakwater at a time when offshore gambling vessels reported calm seas, light local winds, and the lifeguards in the area reported no unusual waves. Massive stones armoring the breakwater weighing from four to 20 tons, that had been in place for years, were dislodged by 12-foot-high waves. While unresolved at the time, it was later discovered that a very long-period southern hemisphere swell had passed between the offshore Channel Islands and over a large hump in the bottom topography. The shallower sea floor over this mound served to focus the long period but only two-foot-high waves into 12-foot damaging breakers when they reached the breakwater (Figure 82).

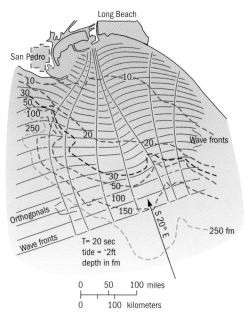

Figure 82. Seafloor bathymetry offshore of Long Beach showing how wave refraction can concentrate wave energy at the end of the harbor breakwater. Dashed lines are bottom contours. Solid lines are wave crests, and solid lines labeled orthogonals are "rays" or energy pathways showing the convergence of wave energy. Adapted from Waves and Beaches, Willard Bascom.

The opposite situation, or the dispersal of wave energy over a depression or deep area in the bottom topography, also occurs frequently. Monterey Submarine Canyon heads into the center of Monterey Bay almost into the Moss Landing harbor (Figure 83). Within the bay, the canyon is considerably deeper than the continental shelf to either side, which causes the wave fronts to bend or refract away from the

Figure 83. The presence of deep water at the head of Monterey Submarine Canyon directly offshore from the entrance to Moss Landing Harbor in Central Monterey Bay leads to wave crests diverging away from the shoreline at this location. Large waves and a broad surf zone occur both north and south of the harbor entrance, but in the area from the entrance to the small pier, wave energy is reduced and the width of the surf zone is quite narrow. Photo California Department of Boating and Waterways.

Figure 84. A Reflected wave colliding with an incoming wave. Photo Gary Griggs.

canyon head so that even when there are large waves within the bay breaking along the shoreline to the north and south, the entrance to the harbor and shoreline in the immediate vicinity is relatively calm (Figure 83).

Wave Reflection: Reversing Energy Flow

Whenever an incoming wave strikes a vertical or near vertical feature, whether natural or artificial, the wave will be reflected off of that surface. Perhaps the easiest to observe are those waves that impact vertical cliffs where there is no protective beach. Depending upon the size of the incoming waves, the reflected wave will move seaward until it collides with the next incoming wave (Figure 84). When the waves are large this collision can create a dramatic vertical explosion of water. On a smaller scale, when a beach scarp has been formed in the beach face due to suddenly changing wave conditions (Figure 85), often in early winter, and the incoming broken wave hits this low vertical scarp, a low wave will be reflected back offshore.

A large and often dangerous example of reflected waves occurs under the right conditions at The Wedge, adjacent to the north jetty at the entrance to Newport Harbor in

Figure 85. Two beach scarps at Natural Bridges State Beach, an older higher scarp and a fresh lower scarp. Photo Gary Griggs

Orange County. The Wedge is popular with boogie boarders and body surfers during a large south swell. Under the right conditions the waves will reflect off the rock jetty and when they meet the large incoming waves they form even larger peaks or a wedge. The wave typically breaks in very shallow water making riding these waves extremely dangerous, even for the experienced surfer. This section of beach has unfortunately been the site of a number of spinal injuries from inexperienced or uninformed swimmers who end up going over the falls and hitting their head on the sand in very shallow water.

In recent years, concern has been widely expressed about the impacts of waves reflecting off of seawalls on adjacent beaches. Waves will reflect off of any vertical or near vertical surface, whether a cliff, a seawall, or even a revetment. Repeated observations and surveys of beaches fronting seawalls and revetments where there are large sand supplies and high littoral drift rates, however, don't indicate that wave reflection has a significant effect on the beaches fronting those walls. Waves are certainly reflected off of seawalls, as they are from cliffs, but no evidence to date has been gathered that shows beach elevations are significantly lower in front of seawalls.

Wave Diffraction: Spreading out the Energy

Wave diffraction is a little less obvious than wave refraction or reflection. Perhaps the best way to think about diffraction is to envision an ocean swell or set of waves moving across the sea surface and then encountering an island. Boats often anchor in the lee of islands, or on the protected side, away from the wind and waves. It must be calmer here, but is this side of an island completely calm? Because of wave diffraction it usually is not. As waves pass around the ends of an island, some of that energy is propagated sideways as the energy of the wave spreads out behind the island (Figure 86). These diffracted wave heights are much less than the original waves, and the area will be more protected, but it will not be completely calm or smooth. Wave diffraction is also a concern inside of some ports and harbors. Although breakwaters and

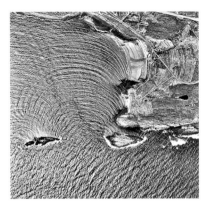

Figure 86. Wave diffraction along the northern coast of Norway.

Figure 87. Wave diffraction behind the breakwater at Ventura Harbor. Photo California Department of Boating and Waterways.

jetties have been designed to protect harbors and harbor entrances, there are examples where waves from certain directions have been diffracted and have set up larger than expected waves inside the harbor, thus damaging boats (Figure 87). The solution has often been to extend a jetty or build an additional segment of breakwater to reduce the extent of diffraction.

Should California Worry About Tsunamis?

Tsunami! The word evokes an instant emotional response for most of us, much like earthquake, or shark! The 2004 earthquake and tsunami in the Indian Ocean, that may have killed 275,000 people, was a recent and tragic reminder of what can happen when waves 30 feet high wash over a densely populated coastline (Figure 88).

Figure 88. Tsunami damage at Banda Aceh from December 26, 2004, earthquake and tsunami. Photo Guy Gelfenbaum, United States Geological Survey.

Just as you can make little ripples by shaking a bowl of water or create small waves by jumping into a swimming pool, any large disturbance or sudden movement under or in the ocean can also generate waves. Enormous oscillations of water caused by large underwater earthquakes, seafloor landslides, or exploding undersea volcanoes result in waves known as tsunamis, or seismic sea waves. These waves have often been incorrectly called tidal waves, but they don't have anything to do with the tides. The word *tsunami* is derived from two Japanese words: "*tsu*," which means harbor, and "*nami*," which means wave. Some of the greatest historical impacts of tsunamis have occurred in harbors or port cities where the wave energy has been concentrated. Hilo, Hawaii, is a good example. Situated at the end of a narrow bay on the big island of Hawaii, in the middle of the Pacific, it has been repeatedly damaged by tsunamis from distant earthquakes. Many of the world's most damaging tsunamis have originated at trenches or subduction zones. It is at these locations where Earth's largest earthquakes occur when oceanic plates descend beneath overlying continental plates. All but a few of Earth's subduction zones occur around the margins of the Pacific Ocean—what has been called the "Ring of Fire"—and this is where many of the world's very large earthquakes and damaging tsunamis have originated. And Hawaii, particularly Hilo, is right in their path.

Everything about tsunamis can be described in superlatives. In the open sea, these waves will typically travel at speeds of 450 or 500 miles per hour, but with heights of only several feet, they are almost imperceptible, and of no real concern to ships at sea. The wavelength of a tsunami, or the distance between two crests, is typically 90 to 100 miles. Recall from earlier in this chapter that waves begin to interact with, or feel the bottom, when the water depth is about one-half of their wavelength. For a tsunami, with a wavelength of 100 miles, this means that the wave feels the bottom when the water depth is less than 50 miles. Since the greatest ocean depth is about seven miles, this means that tsunamis are feeling bottom everywhere. Even though they are influenced by the seafloor throughout the oceans, they still travel at very high velocities. As tsunamis move into the shallow waters near the coastline, the continental shelf acts like a ramp, and their heights increase dramatically.

Even though tsunami speed and wavelength are reduced as they cross the continental shelf, they still have so much mass and momentum that these waves will wash inland a significant distance and also rise to considerable elevations. During the very large 2004 Indian Ocean earthquake and tsunami, waves washed inland for over two miles and at least one of the three waves was 80 feet in height (Figure 89). Tsunamis that have struck the coasts of Japan, Alaska, and Chile over the past 50 years have also reached elevations of

Figure 89. Large boat carried inland at Banda Aceh during the 2006 Indian Ocean tsunami. Photo Guy Gelfenbaum, United States Geological Survey.

over 100 feet above sea level and have swept thousands of feet inland.

Tsunamis can reach the coast of California from any of the trenches or subduction zones that nearly encircle the Pacific Ocean, from the Aleutians south to Chile and from New Zealand north to Kamchatka. So, although these long-period waves might have traveled thousands of miles across the ocean from their source, because of the energy they carry, they can move inland great distances, extend to considerable elevations above sea level, and cause massive damage and loss of life. The closest "local" source for a large tsunami is the Cascadia Subduction Zone that extends from offshore Cape Mendocino to about Vancouver Island (Figure 62).

Discoveries over the past 20 years by field geologists studying preserved sediments along the coastlines of northern California (in the area between Eureka and Crescent City), Oregon, and Washington have provided evidence of a large tsunami that struck this area about 300 years ago. This offshore area is a boundary where one small plate, the Juan de Fuca, collides with the huge North American Plate and is forced down beneath the continent. As the Juan de Fuca Plate slowly descends, there is tremendous friction to a depth of several hundred miles as it scrapes against the bottom of the North American Plate. Most of the time these two plates are locked, but when the accumulated stress is great enough for the two plates to shift and uncouple, the edges of these plates will rebound and a very large amount of energy is released. The rebounding of a massive slab of seafloor when the plates detach displaces a large amount of ocean water, which typically produces a large set of waves or a tsunami.

There is mounting evidence along the coastline of the Pacific Northwest that very large sea floor earthquakes (magnitude 9) and resultant tsunamis occur every several hundred years in the offshore area between Cape Mendocino and Puget Sound. Some of the newer discoveries suggest that these huge waves moved a considerable distance inland into bays and estuaries and left behind beach sands within the muddy organic material that would normally be deposited in these more protected environments. In addition, during a major earthquake of this type, a large portion of sea floor and shoreline may suddenly move upward or downward. Large fir trees that formerly lived a few feet above sea level have been submerged and died when their roots came into contact with salt water. The growth rings on these old trees can be counted, and the age of the trees can also be documented using carbon-14 dating. From a number of investigations of this sort—studying the sediments left behind, the trees that died, and the ages of these materials—we have good evidence that large-magnitude earthquakes occur along the Cascadia Subduction Zone about every 300 years or so on average.

Scientists have also recently uncovered written records 4,500 miles away on the opposite side of the North Pacific providing evidence that the last major earthquake on the Cascadia Subduction Zone generated a tsunami on January 26, 1700, that reached the coast of Japan. Confirming this date, and knowing that great Cascadia earthquakes and tsunamis occur about every 300 years, has significantly increased our level of awareness and concern about when another earthquake of this magnitude will occur, and how the associated tsunami would impact a shoreline that, although still relatively undeveloped, is home to many thousands of people who were not here in 1700.

The California Office of Emergency Services, working with other state and federal agencies, has been developing tsunami risk or inundation maps for the populated areas of the northern California coastline. Oregon's low-lying coastal communities have now posted tsunami warning signs in the lower areas of these towns (Figure 90). Because the Cascadia Subduction Zone is less than 100 miles offshore, however, any earthquake announcement would provide very little warning time to coastal residents.

Figure 90. Tsunami warning sign. Photo Gary Griggs.

Over the past nearly 200 years of somewhat reliable news reporting in California, there have been 13 to 14 tsunamis recorded with heights of over three feet; six of these have been considered destructive. Over this almost 200-year period, about 16 lives have been lost due to tsunamis, far less than the number of people killed by dog bites. The earliest reported event was in 1812, when a tsunami caused by an earthquake in the Santa Barbara Channel generated large waves that washed ashore at Santa Barbara and further west at Gaviota and Refugio canyons. Heights are not known for certain, but based on the scattered descriptions, the distances that the waves washed inland, and the damage left behind, they may have been 10 to 12 feet high.

A tsunami that appears to have been generated by an offshore earthquake hit the coast of Los Angeles, Orange, and San Diego counties in August 1930. Maximum wave heights appear to have been 10 feet, or perhaps higher; many swimmers were rescued and one person is reported to have drowned along the Santa Monica shoreline.

The tsunamis that have been the most damaging to the California coast were both generated by large earthquakes in the Aleutian Trench off of Alaska, one on April Fool's Day in 1946 and the other on Good Friday in 1964. The 1946 tsunami had modest impacts from Noyo Harbor in the north, where many boats broke from their moorings, to Santa Catalina Island in the south. One man walking along the shoreline in Santa Cruz was drowned when the water level rose quickly to 10 feet above normal. In Half Moon Bay, which sits at a very low elevation, 14-foot waves washed a quarter mile inland and damaged houses, boats, and docks.

The most recent and most destructive historic tsunami to batter California's coast accompanied the great, magnitude-9.2, 1964 Alaskan earthquake. Crescent City, on the northern California coast, was the hardest hit, being inundated by a series of waves that pushed buildings off

Figure 91. High water mark in Crescent City from 1964 tsunami where 11 people lost their lives. The blue line on the sign on the right side of the photo marks inundation level. Photo Gary Griggs.

their foundations and into other structures, and swept vehicles and buildings into the ocean. Wave run-up extended 800 to 2,000 feet inland in the commercial and residential areas of the city, with water depths of up to eight feet in city streets and 13 feet along the shoreline (Figure 91). The worst waves struck the waterfront area at 1:45 A.M., drowning 11 people, demolishing 150 stores, and littering the streets with huge redwood logs from a nearby sawmill. Most of the city's downtown was either damaged or totally destroyed (Figure 92), and rather than being rebuilt, the blocks nearest the harbor were subsequently made into a park. According to the U.S. Army Corps of Engineers, property losses approached $187 million (all figures given in 2008 dollars).

To the south, damages from the tsunami ranged from several million dollars at Noyo Harbor in Mendocino

Figure 92. Mural on side of building in Crescent City depicting 1964 tsunami damage. Photo Deepika Shrestha Ross.

County where 100 boats were damaged and 10 to 20 sunk, to $6 million in San Francisco Bay, where docks and boats suffered considerable damage, especially in San Rafael. In Half Moon Bay, Santa Cruz, Avila, and Morro Bay, boats broke loose, were damaged, and sank. Boats and harbor facilities were also damaged in Santa Monica and Los Angeles harbors, where total damages reached about $2 million. There is a pattern here, where nearly all the significant damage was in or adjacent to ports or harbors, where the wave energy can be focused.

The size and impact of a tsunami can vary widely depending on the magnitude of the earthquake, the nature of the offshore bathymetry, the geometry of the shoreline, and the coastal topography. Because most tsunamis approaching the coast of California have come from either Alaskan or South or Central American source areas, they must pass over many miles of shallow continental shelf before they reach the coastline. As a result, wave energy is significantly reduced, and damage has historically been far less when compared with many other areas around the Pacific basin.

Although destructive tsunamis are not everyday events in California, they do occur and will occur in the future. Six destructive tsunamis have reached the California coast over the past 200 years and about 16 lives have been lost. The tsunamis of 1946 and 1964 caused the most damage and are good indicators of what might happen in the future. The highest likelihood event in the decades ahead for producing significant damage is probably a very large earthquake on the Cascadia Subduction Zone, which would no doubt seriously impact the northern California coastline with very little warning time.

What Is It about Beaches?

For many Californians, our beaches define the state and serve as the destinations for our weekends or summer vacations. They are at the center of a lifestyle that has been glamorized and romanticized for decades. People come here from across the country and around the world to visit our beaches, walk in the sand, wade into the water, and maybe buy a T-shirt that says SANTA CRUZ — SURF CITY, USA, for a relative back home.

If you stop and think about it for a minute, what would the coast of California be like without beaches? Perhaps one long highway filled with cars, parking lots, and overlooks for getting a view of the coastline. But the beaches provide us all with many different opportunities, swimming, surfing, jogging, and walking, the list is almost endless, which is why millions of people visit them each year. Beaches only exist, however, because of a unique combination of mineral properties and wave energy. Although there are beaches scattered along California's coast that are made up of large cobbles, pebbles, or shells, these are generally not the places where people spread their towels, play volleyball, or take long quiet walks. It just is not that comfortable lying or walking on shells or baseball-size cobbles (Figure 93).

The ideal beach for most of us consists of fine- to medium-grained white sand and, other than perhaps getting too hot on some long summer days, is perfect for walking, running, sitting, volleyball, and even soccer. What is interesting and what makes beaches around the world possible is that many rocks, granite in particular, consists of minerals that tend to break down over time into sand. Either through physical or chemical weathering in the watersheds or stream channels, or along the shoreline, these rocks decompose and wear down into small, individual mineral grains, quartz and feldspar among the hardest and the most abundant. Rivers

Figure 93. A beach consisting of granitic cobbles along the Monterey Peninsula. Photo Gary Griggs.

can easily transport sand downstream toward the shoreline, and waves are then able to further move these small grains around, sorting and rounding them until they are perfect to walk on. What if most rocks instead broke down into marble or golf ball sized fragments, and this was what we found on most beaches? Well, we do find beaches like this, and they are interesting and different, but they are not usually covered with people, except perhaps in northern Europe.

Beaches: Keeping in Shape

Beaches form where a healthy supply of sand has been delivered to the shoreline, where the coastal topography or bathymetry (the underwater topography) is flat enough that sand has a place to accumulate, and where wave energy is not so high that that sand cannot settle out. Because California is still geologically quite young, and therefore very active, the presence of rising mountains and steep cliffs at some locations (Big Sur, portions of the Mendocino and Humboldt coasts, and the Santa Monica Mountains coast, for example) have not allowed space or time for beaches to form. Many of the state's scenic and secluded pocket beaches have formed where streams have cut through the coastal mountains or sea cliffs, or where waves have eroded embayments or small coves in the weaker materials making up the coastline.

Long, straight or gently curved beaches, often backed by sand dunes, form where there are no mountains or steep cliffs, where the coastline relief is low and ample sand is available. These are usually the beaches that many residents, visitors, and the movie industry envision when they picture the California coast, a wide sandy beach lined by palm trees and convertibles. Somewhat fortuitously, many of the state's most extensive sandy beaches are in southern California, where most of the state's population is concentrated and the weather is the warmest. These include the long sandy stretch of shoreline from Santa Monica to Redondo Beach (Figure 94), the coast from Huntington Beach to Newport, and the white sands of the Silver Strand in San Diego. Far

Figure 94. A wide, sandy beach at Santa Monica. Photo Kenneth and Gabrielle Adelman, California Coastal Records Project, www. CaliforniaCoastline.org.

Figure 95. Monterey Bay contains two long, gently curving sandy shorelines that converge at Moss Landing in the center of the bay. Photo NASA.

to the north, Monterey Bay is a 30-mile-long, gently curved section of sandy shoreline that extends from Santa Cruz to Monterey (Figure 95), and that, despite its chilly water, attracts millions of central California visitors and residents annually. Not surprisingly, these long, wide stretches of beach are very important income generators for local economies.

Beaches form upcoast of many natural headlands along the California coastline. Rocky points or other obstructions trap the sand moving along the shoreline and thereby create or widen the beaches next to these barriers. Point Dume, for example, along the Malibu coast, has led to the formation of the mile-long Zuma and Broad beaches (Figure 96).

Figure 96. Point Dume is a prominent headland that has trapped littoral drift coming from upcoast to form Zuma and Broad beaches. Photo Bruce Perry, CSULB Geological Sciences.

A few miles to the west, Point Mugu has a similar effect and has trapped enough sand to form a beach nearly two miles long. Morro Rock in San Luis Obispo County has also trapped the sand moving southward along the shoreline, forming an extensive beach. In the city of Santa Cruz, San Lorenzo Point is a natural rock outcrop that has led to the formation of Main Beach, a three-quarter-mile-long wide strip of sand that has been a popular recreation area and home to the Santa Cruz Beach Boardwalk for over a century (Figure 97).

Jetties, groins, and breakwaters also serve as obstructions to sand transport along the shoreline. They have either created beaches where none previously existed, or stabilized or expanded existing but narrow beaches. Groins essentially replicate small natural points or headlands, and are built with the specific purpose of stabilizing, widening, or building beaches. This achieves several benefits: more beach area is available for recreation, and greater protection is provided from winter wave attack for

Figure 97. San Lorenzo Point, adjacent to the mouth of the San Lorenzo River in Santa Cruz, forms an obstruction to littoral drift that has led to the formation of Main Beach. Immediately down coast, the jetty of the Santa Cruz Small Craft Harbor has trapped sand to widen Seabright Beach. Photo California Dept. of Boating and Waterways.

any backshore bluffs, dunes, development, or infrastructure. Although there are important benefits of constructing groins, and they have been used by the Army Corps of Engineers for decades, there are usually potential impacts. By trapping sand behind the groins, the shoreline further down the coast will initially be deprived of sand and the beaches may narrow or the coastline may experience increased erosion. The number, length, spacing, and height of groins are all important considerations, as is the need to fill the groins with sand from another source at the time of their emplacement so as not to generate erosion problems downcoast. Groups of groins have been effectively used for years to stabilize the beaches at Ventura, Santa Monica, and Newport Beach (Figure 98), which attract thousands

Figure 98. Groins along the Santa Monica coast have widened this stretch of beach by trapping sand moving from top to bottom. Photo Bruce Perry, CSULB Geological Sciences.

of visitors. At Capitola, a single groin has worked effectively to widen and stabilize that community's main beach for 40 years (Figure 99).

Breakwaters and jetties are designed and constructed for different purposes, usually to provide a protected anchorage for boats or a safe entrance channel to a harbor or marina. Although these structures are not intended to trap sand, because they usually extend so far offshore, they are responsible for disrupting the littoral transport of sand along the shoreline and form wide beaches. Nearly every pair of jetties and every breakwater constructed along the state's coastline have built a large beach. The width of the beach and the distance that the beach extends up or downcoast is directly related to how far offshore the structure extends. Beaches extend for miles both up and downcoast from the 4,000-foot-long jetties at Humboldt Bay. The west jetty of the small craft harbor at Santa Cruz has trapped enough sand to build a wide beach that extends more than a mile upcoast (Figure 100). Breakwaters and jetties at Santa

Figure 99. A rock groin was built in Capitola in 1969 to help rebuild a beach that was lost when the Santa Cruz small craft harbor was built upcoast. Photo California Dept. of Boating and Waterways.

Figure 100. The west jetty of the small craft harbor at Santa Cruz trapped hundreds of thousands of cubic yards of sand moving along the shoreline to widen Seabright Beach by about 400 feet. Photo Gary Griggs.

Barbara, Ventura, Channel Islands, Port Hueneme, Marina del Rey, Balboa Bay, and Oceanside harbors have had similar effects, widening the upcoast beaches, but often producing downcoast erosion problems, with many of these harbors requiring annual dredging to keep the flow of sand moving (Figure 101).

A satellite view or high altitude aerial photograph of the California coast reveals some perfectly curved sections of shoreline. Half Moon Bay, south of San Francisco, was named after its smooth, natural curve, although this shape was altered following the construction of a massive breakwater

Figure 101. About 200,000 to 250,000 cubic yards of sand must be dredged from the mouth of the Santa Cruz Harbor each year. Photo Gary Griggs.

Figure 102. Half Moon Bay was originally a perfect hook shaped bay. After the breakwater and harbor were completed in 1959, the wave energy was concentrated at the end of the breakwater where bluff erosion was accelerated. Photo California Dept. of Boating and Waterways.

in 1959, which completely changed where and how the waves break (Figure 102). Shelter Cove, Drakes Bay, Stinson Beach, both ends of Monterey Bay, Coronado (Figure 103), and San Pedro Bay in its pre-breakwater configuration, are other examples of shorelines that originally or still do have a nearly perfect hooked shape. These bays begin with a tight curve downcoast of a point or headland, and then gradually uncoil proceeding alongshore, just like the shell of an abalone or other mollusk as it grows. These uncoiling shorelines owe

Figure 103. The shoreline from Imperial Beach to Coronado is a very smooth curve or hook shape. Photo Bruce Perry, CSULB Geological Sciences.

their origin to the process of wave refraction, and form where rocks occur along the coast that differ in their resistance to wave attack. Where a hard rocky headland exists in the midst of otherwise weaker or more erodible rocks, and there is a dominant direction of wave approach, the stage is set for the formation of one of these uniquely shaped sections of shoreline. Half Moon Bay is a good example, where Pillar Point stands out as a major rocky headland standing 150 feet above sea level. As the dominant waves approach from the northwest, they first break at Mavericks and then wrap around Pillar Point and begin to attack the low-lying and softer sedimentary rocks immediately downcoast. The bending or refraction of the waves as they wrap around the point spreads out or diffuses the wave energy in a very regular pattern. These refracted waves gradually erode the weaker rocks downcoast from the point and, over time, the shoreline or beach will gradually begin to develop a gently curved or uncoiling shape that mirrors the wave fronts of the refracted waves (Figure 104).

Figure 104. Morro Rock, near the town of Morro Bay in San Luis Obispo County, is connected to the shoreline by a sandspit or tombolo. Photo California Dept. of Boating and Waterways. The shoreline behind the breakwaters parallels the wave fronts.

California does not have the long, narrow sandy barrier islands that lie offshore and buffer most of the Gulf and south Atlantic states from hurricane attack. Fire Island, Padre Island, the Outer Banks, Roanoke, Canaveral, Palm Beach, and Chincoteague, are just a few of these sandy barriers that have been regularly overwashed by hurricanes, but in many cases have also been extensively developed. Our offshore continental shelf is steeper and narrower and our wave energy is usually greater, such that conditions were not right for the formation of these sandy barriers. What California does have are sand spits or barrier bars, which enclose a number of bays or estuaries (Figure 105). So rather than offshore islands, these accumulations of sand are connected at one end, or both in some cases, to the shoreline, and may extend for thousands of feet parallel to the coast. These sand spits or bars require low lying coastal topography, large volumes of sand, transport of that sand alongshore by wave action, and

Figure 105. Big Lagoon, along the Humboldt County coastline, is completely separated from the ocean by a 3.5-mile-long sand spit. Photo Kenneth and Gabrielle Adelman, California Coastal Records Project, www.CaliforniaCoastline.org.

may form initially where a river discharges. The river course at its mouth may be deflected upcoast or downcoast by the dominant littoral drift of sand, which will begin to form a sand bar or a beach, separated from the land by the river outlet (Figure 106).

There are many of these elongate sand spits or barrier beaches, although we may not immediately recognize them. Coronado and the Silver Strand is a long sand spit stretching from Imperial Beach northward to the Zuniga jetty that separates San Diego Bay from the ocean. To the north, Agua Hedionda Lagoon, Balboa Bay, Bolsa Chica, Goleta Beach, and Morro Bay are all locations along the south coast where sand spits have formed (Figure 107), some short and some long, some developed and some undeveloped. Along the central and north coast, Moss Landing, Stinson Beach, Bodega Bay, Gualala, the Eel River, Humboldt Bay, Big Lagoon, Stone Lagoon, Lake Earl, and the mouth of the Smith River all have well-developed sand spits. In some unique cases, Morro Rock, Pt. Sur, Greyhound Rock, and Goat Rock, for example,

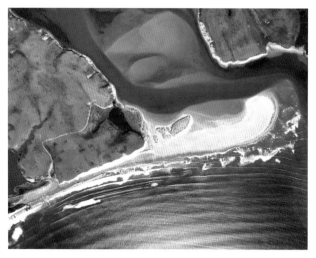

Figure 106. A long, curved sand spit has formed by sand moving from left to right (west to east) across a lagoon in Drake's Bay in Marin County. Photo California Dept. of Boating and Waterways.

Figure 107. A sand spit has formed across the entrance to a lagoon north of Solana Beach in northern San Diego County. Photo California Dept. of Boating and Waterways.

Figure 108. Point Sur is a massive rock headland connected to the Big Sur coastline by a sand spit or tombolo. Photo Kenneth and Gabrielle Adelman, California Coastal Records Project, www.CaliforniaCoastline.org.

long sand spits have grown over time and now connect or tie very large rock sea stacks to the shoreline (Figures 104 and 108). These sandy connections are known as tombolos.

Where Does All the Beach Sand Come From?

Waves create most of California's beaches from the sand that creeks and rivers deliver to the coast during winter storms. The finer silt and clay are carried offshore and may be transported hundreds of miles by ocean currents before finally settling onto the seafloor somewhere. These small particles are simply too fine-grained and too light to be stable on a beach, even under low wave energy conditions. Although we can find silt or clay on the mudflats of an estuary or protected bay, we will not find them on any of the state's open coast beaches.

Figure 109. Polished gravel on Pebble Beach along the San Mateo coastline. Photo Gary Griggs.

We do have pebble, cobble, and shell beaches along California's coast, and in fact they are often named after these coarse materials because they are so unique or different: Pebble Beach, Shell Beach, or Sand Dollar Beach, for example, and we even have a Glass Beach for Fort Bragg. Because they are so different, they typically attract lots of visitors who often load up their pockets or containers with the shells or pebbles. Pebble Beach along the San Mateo coast (Figure 109) is a good example, where park staff finally had to post a sign asking people to restrict their removal of the beautiful shiny pebbles from the beach. These coarse beaches usually form under some unique set of conditions. The rocks in the surrounding cliffs may consist of pebbles, for example, or there may not be a nearby source of sand. In other places, the wave energy is so high that sand is not stable on the beach, or perhaps the area is a rich habitat for clams or sand dollars or some other shellfish such that their shells accumulate on the shoreline. In the tropics, most of the beaches are made up of shells such as mollusks, bryozoans, and lots of others, as well as coral, simply because there usually is not much or any river-supplied sand around to build a beach.

Even sandy beaches, however, can look very different in California depending upon the types of minerals in the sand. Most of our beaches tend to be white, very light gray, or tan, which usually reflects the relative amounts of quartz and feld-spar, the two most common beach-forming minerals. Both of these minerals are major constituents of granitic rocks and are quite resistant to breakdown, so they survive the weathering and transport processes to end up on our beaches. Quartz is a clear or glassy mineral and quartz-rich beaches, like that at Carmel, tend to be white in appearance. A higher content of feldspar will produce a gray- or tan-colored beach sand.

We also have black, green, and even pink sand beaches. Black sand is common on a number of central and northern California beaches, and is usually more abundant in the winter months, when the more common quartz and feldspar on the surface of the beach have been eroded or scoured away, leaving the heavier black sand behind. The black or dark minerals, such as magnetite, ilmenite, and chromite, can be separated from the lighter-colored sand by a hand magnet as you used to do in the sand box as a child. These dark minerals contain heavy elements such as iron, titanium, and magnesium, and these denser grains are left behind by the winter waves as they remove the lower density quartz and feldspar grains. The black sand will often be concentrated in small rills, channels, or in the troughs of the ripples on the beach surface (Figure 110). For a short while in the 1920s, the Triumph Steel Company owned nearly two miles of beach along the northern Monterey Bay shoreline and was mining the black sand, which contained 500 to 1,100

Figure 110. Black and pink sands consist of heavier minerals that are concentrated in drainage channels or rills on the beach. Photo Gary Griggs.

pounds of magnetite per ton of sand. They used a magnetic separator to remove the magnetite and then used a furnace to produce a red iron oxide that was used in the manufacture of paint. While this could have happened in the 1920s, mining beach sand from a public beach and setting up a furnace on the beach would probably not be viewed very favorably today.

There are also some green minerals, amphibole and pyroxene, for example, which are common in granitic rocks, and olivine, common in some volcanic rocks, and these may also be concentrated on certain beaches to give them a dark green color. Near the mouth of the Big Sur River, which is a pleasant hike from State Hwy. 1 through Andrew Molera State Park, you can find sections of the rugged and scenic beach south of the river mouth that are pink due to the high concentration of the mineral garnet (Figure 111). Garnet is a very hard, reddish colored mineral that is derived from a garnet-rich rock in the Big Sur River watershed. Being very resistant to wear, this mineral persists in the beach sand, and because of its hardness, is also a mineral commonly used in sandpaper.

Beach glass has become a popular collector's item and small amounts of it can be found on a number of California's pebble or coarse sandy beaches. One of the coves along the coast of Wilder Ranch State Park, just north of the city of Santa Cruz, was for years used as the dump for broken bottles

Figure 111. Garnet sand can be found at the mouth of the Big Sur River in Molera State Park in Monterey County. Photo Deepika Shrestha Ross.

and other debris from the old ranch. Although the trash was removed when the ranch became a state park, small pieces of the worn and polished glass can still be found in the winter months on the adjacent beaches. Perhaps the best example is Glass Beach, just north of the town of Fort Bragg on the Mendocino coast. A section of low coastline was used for many years as the city dump, and as the waves worked and reworked the glass and ceramic, they have left behind a beach that consists primarily of green, brown, blue, and clear glass that sparkles when wet (Figure 112), and that has attracted visitors and collectors for years.

Though there are these scattered locations along our coast where the material on the beach has come from a local trash dump or perhaps a nearshore shell bed, most of California's beach sand comes from two sources: streams or local bluff erosion. Measurements of sediment transport in rivers indicate that coastal streams, particularly during times of flood, are the major suppliers of sand to our beaches. Physical and chemical weathering slowly break down rocks in the coastal mountains or watersheds into smaller fragments or into their constituent mineral grains. Rainfall, landslides, and runoff begin to move the gravel, sand, silt, and clay downslope into the creeks, where they are gradually sorted out and transported

Figure 112. Glass Beach at Fort Bragg consists largely of worn and polished glass from an old beach dump. Photo Deepika Shrestha Ross.

downstream into the larger rivers. After many months and miles of abrasion and sorting, the smaller particles ultimately reach the shoreline whereas the larger boulders and cobbles have been left behind upstream. The sand and gravel end up on the beach, and the silt and clay are carried offshore.

California is fortunate to have many rivers that deliver large quantities of sand to the coastline to nourish our beaches. The Eel, Russian, Santa Maria, Ventura, and Santa Clara rivers are all important sand suppliers to the northern and central California shoreline. Southern California gets much less rain, the rivers are much smaller, and many, like the Los Angeles, San Gabriel, and Santa Ana rivers, no longer look or even behave like rivers. They have been dammed, mined for sand and gravel, and their downstream sections have been converted into concrete lined channels (Figure 113). Under natural conditions, California's rivers, large and small, delivered about 13 million cubic yards of sand to the coastline each year, on average. The construction

Figure 113. Ballona Creek is now a concrete channel that empties into Santa Monica next to Marina del Rey. Photo Bruce Perry, CSULB Geological Sciences.

of nearly 500 dams on the coastal rivers over the past 125 years, however, has significantly impacted this beach sand delivery (see subsequent discussion).

Beaches are usually much wider in summers following winters with high rainfall because of the delivery of large amounts of sand to the coast by floods. Sediment transport by rivers to California's shoreline is extremely episodic, however, with most of the sediment transported during a few days each year. Years with little rainfall and low river flows don't contribute sand to the beaches. Sediment discharge during a single year of extreme flood conditions may exceed decades of low or normal river flow, like in 1969, when over 100 million tons of sediment (about 7.5 million dump truck loads) was flushed out of the Santa Ynez Mountains. That was more than the previous 25 years combined! Even more amazing, in a single day during a large flood on December 23, 1964, the Eel River in northern California transported 57 million tons

Figure 114. The failure and erosion of the steep, high cliffs at Torrey Pines contributes sand to the beach. Photo Kenneth and Gabrielle Adelman, California Coastal Records Project, www.CaliforniaCoastline.org.

of sediment (about 4.2 million dump truck loads), which represented nearly 20 percent of the sediment load carried by the river over the previous 10 years! When large dams are constructed, they trap the sand and virtually eliminate these floods, which provide most of the sand to California's beaches.

Where coastal cliffs are sandy, which is the case along the northern San Diego coast, they may also be important local sources of beach sand (Figure 114). Overall, however, cliffs probably provide no more than 10 to 15 percent of the beach sand in most areas. It is really California's rivers and streams that are responsible for the sand on our beaches.

No Time for Rest: Beach Sand in Motion

Those wide sandy summer beaches look pretty stable and permanent, but the sand rarely sits still for very long. Wind blows the sand around on the back-beach, and the waves are constantly at work pushing the sand back and forth, across and along the beach face. Every time the tide goes in and out and each time we have a winter storm, the shape of the shoreline will change. These daily and seasonal processes and a number of other subtle and more obvious features are easily recognized by coastal residents, frequent beach visitors, or a careful observer.

Here Today, Gone Tomorrow: Seasonal Beach Changes

Perhaps the most striking, noticeable change to the shape of most beaches is that which takes place between winter and summer. The summer beach has a berm, which is the wide, dry, higher part of the beach where we throw our towels, have

Figure 115A. Boardwalk Beach in Santa Cruz in the summer. Photo Gary Griggs.

picnics, and perhaps play Frisbee or volleyball (Figure 115A). The berm may be hundreds of feet wide. In winter, all or much of this sand is removed by the steeper and more energetic waves, usually leaving behind a much narrower winter berm (Figure 115B). Although the total amount of sand spread

Figure 115B. Boardwalk Beach in Santa Cruz in the winter. Photo Gary Griggs.

between the exposed and submerged part of the beach is about the same in summer and winter, it has been redistributed in response to different wave conditions.

The beach responds to the more energetic winter waves by moving sand offshore, where it usually forms a series of longshore bars, or large sand waves on the seafloor that are parallel to the shoreline, separated by longshore troughs. Because the depth where the waves break is determined by the height of the waves, the presence of these sand bars causes the waves to break farther offshore. This dissipates more of the breaking wave's energy offshore, which reduces the wave energy expended on the beach and acts as a natural shock absorber.

In the late spring and summer months, the less energetic and less steep waves will gradually begin to move the sand that accumulated on the longshore bars back onto the beach. These more gentle waves will wash the sand up the beach face, building up the berm over the months ahead. By July or August the exposed beach will usually be at its maximum width again, in time for all the summer visitors.

The balance between a winter and a summer beach, or the wave conditions that move sand offshore and those that move it onshore, is somewhat delicate, and conditions can change quickly that will reverse the transport of sand. Years of observations as well as experiments in wave tanks have shown that the wave steepness, which is the ratio between the wave height (h) and the wave length (L), or h/L, exerts the strongest influence on whether the sand is moving onshore to form a berm, or offshore to form sand bars. Winter or storm waves tend to be steeper, and are more effective at moving sand off the beach face or berm and transporting it offshore. The less steep summer swells move sand the other way, back onshore to rebuild the berm, providing us a place to sit.

All this back and forth movement of sand grains is brought about by the movement of water or turbulence near the seafloor produced by the passage or breaking of each wave.

Just as you get thrown around when body surfing or playing in the waves, the sand grains are a lot smaller and lighter and are picked up and carried along much easier. Once a sand grain is picked up off the bottom, it is moved with the near-shore currents or by the breaking wave and can be carried a few inches or many feet each time a wave breaks.

During the passage of lower and less steep summer waves, the circular or orbital movement of the water near the seafloor picks up the sand grains and moves them a short distance towards the shoreline with the passage of each wave. Thus there is a net onshore movement of the sand grains, gradually adding sand to the beach face.

With steeper winter waves, however, which break more frequently, the entire surf zone is very turbulent, which keeps the sand stirred up. There is no time for the sand to settle out between waves, and the sand stays in suspension longer. The general pattern seems to be that the water at the surface in the surf zone is moving up the beach face, while the water near the bottom, where most of the sand is concentrated, is moving seaward. This leads to an overall transport of sand off of the beach face and offshore where it will settle out onto the bars that form in the winter or stormy months.

The Coarser the Grains, the Steeper the Beach

If you have ever been to a very coarse-grained beach, one consisting of pebbles or cobbles, you may have noticed that it is usually much steeper than a typical sandy beach (Figure 116). On the other hand, if you have been to a very fine-grained beach, Pismo Beach or San Diego, or perhaps Florida, you will find that these beaches are very flat. In fact, Daytona Beach, Florida, is one of those very fine-grained and flat beaches where cars raced on the beach for over 50 years, and where in some restricted areas vehicles can still drive on the beach today.

Figure 116. A steep cobble beach along the Normandy coast of France. Photo Gary Griggs.

Why are some beaches so steep they are hard to walk on and others are flat enough to race a car on? There is a fairly straightforward relationship: coarse beaches are steeper and fine-grained beaches are flatter. You can observe the process that is responsible for this difference the next time you go to a gravel or cobble beach. When a wave breaks and water surges up the beach face, some of that uprush will percolate into the beach face, and the rest will flow back down the beach as backwash. It is the balance between these two, the flow in the uprush and backwash that exerts the dominant control on the slope of the beach.

Gravel or cobble beach are very permeable and water can flow through them very easily because there are large voids or spaces between the individual stones. As the broken wave runs up the beach, much of that water will percolate into the large voids between the rocks, and the backwash is thus greatly reduced in volume. Thus, the individual stones are carried up the beach face and can remain at a relatively steep slope because there is little backwash to carry the pebbles or cobbles back down the beach face. An analogy exists between this process and throwing a pail full of water against a steep pile of cobbles. Because the stack is so permeable, most of the water will wash into the voids or spaces between the pebbles and the pile will remain pretty much intact.

Now, let us consider a very fine-grained sand beach, the kind of beach you might find at Pismo Beach or Santa Monica, for example, where the grains are a tenth of a millimeter in diameter. When the wave washes up the beach face, the spaces between the grains are very small so that very little of the water can percolate into the sand. So nearly all the uprush returns as backwash. The backwash will carry any sand that is carried up the beach by the incoming wave back down the beach face. The sand thus cannot stand at any significant slope because the backwash volume carries the sand back down the beach. Using the pail of water analogy again, if we throw a pail of water onto a steep pile of very fine sand, we will find that the water cannot penetrate the sand and the sand pile will spread out and gradually form a much flatter slope.

By looking at lots of different beaches, some general relationships have been determined between the average particle size and the slope of the beach face. Very fine-grained or fine-grained sand, (0.10 to 0.25 mm diameter grains) for example, will have very low slopes of a few degrees. Medium-grained sand (0.25 to 0.50 mm) will be steeper, 4 to 6 degrees, and coarse-grained sand beaches (0.50 to 2.0 mm) even steeper, six to 10 degrees or steeper. Pebble and cobble beaches may be 10 to 20 degrees and difficult to walk on (Figure 116). At extreme slopes are riprap revetments, where large boulders are placed against the edge of a bluff or cliff to reduce wave impact or protect property, and may be stacked at over 30 degrees, or the angle of repose.

Going with the Flow: Littoral Drift

Every time a wave breaks it suspends or picks up billions of grains of sand. That sand is not only moved up the beach face, but, depending upon the angle at which the waves approach the coast, the sand may also move along the shoreline, upcoast or downcoast. Most waves approach the shoreline at some angle, simply because the storms that generated the waves were somewhere far out to sea to the north or to the south, but probably not directly offshore. As the waves enter shallow water and begin to feel the bottom (recall that this happens when the water depth is about one-half of the wave length of the waves) that portion of the wave reaching the shallow water first will begin to slow down. The amount of the bending or refraction of the wave front as it approaches the shoreline is related to the original angle of wave approach. Refraction is rarely complete, however, so even when the waves break, they will still often peel off or progressively break at some angle to the shoreline. It is that angle, or difference in orientation between the beach face and the breaking wave, that most strongly affects the movement of sand along the shoreline.

As each wave breaks at an angle to the beach, it stirs up and suspends the sand and washes it up the beach face at a slight angle (Figure 117). The backwash flows back down the beach face at a slight angle, carrying the sand with it. So each wave picks up billions of grains of sand, moves them back and forth across the beach face, and they end up some distance away from where they started, depending upon the angle at which the waves break and the size of the waves. Where the waves break almost parallel to the beach face, the sand will be carried up and down the beach at a very small angle and not move too far with each wave. Where the waves approach and break at a larger angle, however, the transport of the sand grains up the beach face will be at a larger angle and they will be transported a greater distance with each breaking wave.

At first glance, this may not seem like a very effective mechanism for transporting sand, at least compared to a large river in flood stage; so how much sand can this process really move? If we just pick an average wave, say a wave with a period of eight seconds, there will be 450 of these waves breaking every hour, or 10,800 breaking each day! That is a lot of waves. If each wave moves individual sand grains

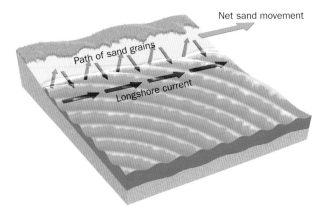

Figure 117. The process of littoral drift moves sand along the shoreline.

only one inch along the shoreline, this amounts to 900 feet of movement along the shoreline each day. So this process that may have seemed unimportant initially is actually very effective after all. Water in the surf zone is often discolored with sediment stirred up by large waves, and once sand is suspended, it can be moved quickly along the shoreline by nearshore currents. If you have spent much time swimming or surfing in the ocean you have probably experienced longshore currents, which you notice when you look up and realize that you've been carried several hundred yards down the beach. The sand is moving at nearly this same rate and for hours or days at a time.

With thousands of waves breaking on the beach every day, the net result is a slowly moving current of water and sand that flows downcoast and parallel to the shoreline, known as a longshore current. Longshore currents exist along most of California's beaches. They are driven by waves breaking at an angle to the beach and are the process that moves sand along the shoreline. This transport of sand along the beach is known as littoral drift, and can be thought of as a river of sand moving parallel to the coast. Hundreds of thousands of cubic yards of sand may travel as littoral drift each year along different sections of California's shoreline. The amount of sand moving along the shore is related to the volume of sand available, the amount of wave energy, and the angle at which waves approach the shoreline, with waves breaking parallel to the beach transporting almost no sand and those breaking at a greater angle transporting more sand.

Because the more energetic and steeper winter waves usually approach from the northwest, the transport of sand along the shoreline is dominantly southward along most of the state's coastline (Figure 118). This is not the case everywhere, however. North of Cape Mendocino, both northerly and southerly transport occurs, and in the extreme southern part of the state, from the Mexican border north to Oceanside, littoral transport to the north takes place frequently.

How much sand is moving along California's coastline? Because harbor mouths typically form nearly complete traps for sand moving alongshore, the average amount of sand dredged from a harbor entrance each year can give us a good idea of how much sand is being carried by waves as littoral drift at that particular location. Sand transport rates along California's coast show a considerable range, not only because of the differences in the waves at any individual location and at any given time, but also because of the amount of sand present to transport. Along the Malibu coast, for example, about 50,000 cubic yards are moved alongshore by the waves in a typical year. Average littoral drift rates of about 300,000 cubic yards per year occur at both Santa Cruz and Santa Barbara, and as much as one million cubic yards per year move along

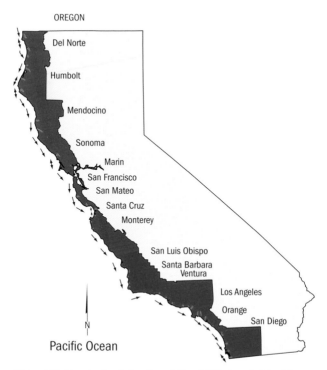

OREGON

Del Norte

Humbolt

Mendocino

Sonoma

Marin

San Francisco

San Mateo

Santa Cruz

Monterey

San Luis Obispo

Santa Barbara
Ventura

Los Angeles

Orange

San Diego

N

Pacific Ocean

Figure 118. The dominant direction of littoral drift along California's coastline is from north to south, although there are some areas of reversal.

the shoreline south of Ventura. Think of these volumes in terms of dump trucks, with a large dump truck carrying about 10 cubic yards. Three hundred thousand cubic yards moving along the shoreline is equivalent to 30,000 dump trucks, or a line of bumper-to-bumper trucks 142 miles long. One million cubic yards a years is harder to envision, but is the equivalent of a line of large dump trucks 475 miles long heading down the beach. There is a huge amount of sand moving almost invisibly along the shoreline as littoral drift, although much of it moves episodically during the storms with the largest waves.

Interrupting or blocking this amount of sand every year can have big and expensive impacts. Imagine the size of a pile of sand that would be formed if a line of trucks 142 miles long, each carrying 10 cubic yards, dumped their loads in one place and how long it would take to move the resulting pile. This is the scenario faced by many of California's harbormasters or port directors where a jetty or a breakwater interrupt the alongshore transport of sand.

Between 1970 and 2001, for example, over 10 million cubic yards of sand were dredged from the Santa Barbara Harbor, nearly 20 million cubic yards were dredged from the Ventura Harbor, and roughly 28 million cubic yards of sand were dredged from the Channel Islands Harbor, at a cost of tens of millions of dollars. Dredging from just these three harbors totaled over 58 million cubic yards, or 5.8 million dump truck loads, of sand over this 31-year period. This line of trucks would extend the entire length of the California coastline from Oregon to the border with Mexico 11 times! These three harbors are just a few of many large sand traps that have been

Figure 119. Annual dredging at the Channel Islands Harbor may remove over a million cubic yards of sand. Photo Kenneth and Gabrielle Adelman, California Coastal Records Project, www.CaliforniaCoastline.org.

created along the coast of California, where jetties and break-waters have been built and where annual dredging is a permanent and expensive way of life (Figure 119).

California's Biggest Sand Boxes: Littoral Cells

Many years of study of the coastline of southern California led to the recognition of a series of distinct beach compartments or littoral cells. These are self-contained segments of the coast characterized by distinct sources of sand, littoral drift of the sand along the shoreline, and sinks or routes where the sand is lost from the cell. It was the discovery of the many offshore submarine canyons and the realization that sand moving downcoast along the beaches was flowing into these canyons that led scientists to this concept. Down drift of many of the canyons, the beaches narrow or disappear and rocky headlands or points typically mark the end of each compartment. Continuing down drift, streams again begin to deliver sand to the shoreline, beaches appear, and as more sand enters the cell, the beaches begin to widen. Proceeding farther down the coast, another submarine canyon intersects the shoreline, the beach sand is conveyed offshore, and the end of another compartment or cell is reached.

Along the southern California coast, between Santa Barbara and San Diego, five distinct littoral cells have been recognized: the Santa Barbara Cell, the Zuma Cell, the Santa Monica Cell, the San Pedro Cell, and the Oceanside Cell (Figure 120). Each is characterized by individual sources of beach sand (primarily streams and bluff erosion), downcoast littoral drift, and a sink or sinks (coastal dunes and submarine canyons). Other littoral cells have been recognized along the entire length of the California coast, although the boundaries and the total volumes of sand moving through these cells are still being measured and documented.

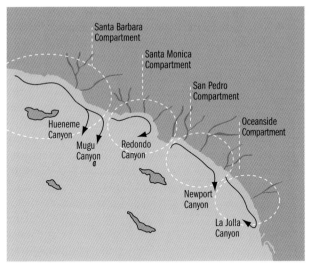

Figure 120. The coastline of southern California can be divided into a number of distinct littoral cells.

Where Does All That Sand Go?

Along most of the state's coastline, the littoral drift is carrying the beach sand southward (Figure 118). Where then, is all this sand going, and why are the beaches not growing wider and wider as you move downcoast? If we follow the paths of typical sand grains, we observe several possible routes by which sand may leave the beach permanently as it moves along the shoreline.

Blowing in the Wind: Sand Losses to Dunes

Dunes occur inland from beaches at many locations along the California coast, and they can act as sinks where beach sand can be permanently lost from the shoreline. As a beach widens and the area of dry sand on the back-beach expands, a persistent onshore wind can begin to move the sand inland and off the beach. As was discussed earlier, large volumes of beach sand historically were blown inland as dunes in places like Ocean Beach in San Francisco (Figure 38), along the southern Monterey Bay shoreline (Figure 36), Pismo Beach and Nipomo Dunes (Figure 37), the Oxnard Plain, and from Santa Monica to El Segundo. Some of these dune areas are very large and account for a lot of lost beach sand.

In addition to the natural process of sand loss through wind blowing onshore, sand was historically mined directly from some California beaches and dunes. Three major sand-mining companies removed sand directly from the beach in southern Monterey Bay for nearly 90 years. The smooth, rounded, amber-colored sand was in great demand for many industrial uses, including water filtration, abrasives, and various coatings. Severe wave erosion of the dunes during the 1980s and early 1990s, however, raised the question of whether the mining of approximately 150,000 to 250,000 cubic yards

Figure 121. Sand is still being dredged from a pond on the back beach in southern Monterey Bay and sold commercially. Photo Kenneth and Gabrielle Adelman, California Coastal Records Project, www .CaliforniaCoastline.org.

of sand from the beach was the cause of the ongoing shoreline retreat. Ultimately all but one beach-sand-mining operation was terminated around 1990. Unfortunately, due to agency jurisdictional issues, the remaining sand company dredges their sand from a back-beach pond (Figure 121), which has continued and at an increased rate of about 235,000 cubic yards each year, while the adjacent shoreline continues to retreat.

Slip Sliding Away: Sand Losses into Submarine Canyons

The greatest loss of sand from California's beaches is invisible to us and occurs down the many submarine canyons that wind their way across the seafloor just offshore. Where these canyons extend close to shore, which they do in many places, they intercept the sand moving along the shoreline and funnel it away from the beach into deep offshore basins (Figure 122).

Figure 122. Submarine canyons in Santa Monica Bay funnel sand offshore where it is transported by turbidity currents to Santa Monica Basin. Image US Geological Survey.

The canyons of southern California have been recognized for over 75 years and are the ultimate sinks for most of southern California's beach sand. Every year on average, the Scripps Submarine Canyon at La Jolla swallows an estimated 275,000 cubic yards of sand, enough to form a beach 10 feet deep, 100 feet wide, and 1.4 miles long. The Mugu Submarine Canyon, south of Ventura, is even more impressive as a sand sink; it siphons off over a million cubic yards of sand each year on average, enough to build a beach 100 feet wide, 10 feet deep, and five miles long. Other offshore canyons remove sand from the coastal sand budget as well; the Dume, Redondo, and Newport submarine canyons play similar roles.

Monterey Submarine Canyon, which bisects Monterey Bay and extends almost to the beach at Moss Landing, is one of the world's largest submarine canyons—over 6,000 feet deep and big enough to hold the Grand Canyon of the Colorado River, but completely invisible to us standing on the beach (Figure 123)! Every year, virtually all the nearly 300,000 cubic yards of sand that

Figure 123. A multibeam image of the head of Monterey Submarine Canyon combined with a LIDAR image of the onshore topography reveal the connection between the shoreline and the canyon head. Image Douglas Smith, Seafloor Mapping Lab, California State University Monterey Bay.

are transported down the coast of northern Monterey Bay, some from as far as 75 miles to the north at Half Moon Bay, as well as the sand carried northward from the Salinas River, are carried off-shore into deep water by this vast underwater conveyor belt.

Once sand starts moving into one of these canyons, it is lost permanently to the beach. Observations by scuba divers and submersibles reveal that in the steeper canyon heads this sand simply flows down slope, grain by grain, the same process that occurs when you start digging into a steep sand dune. Transport farther offshore, however, where the slopes are less severe, is achieved by underwater mudflows known as turbidity currents. Turbidity currents are large masses of sand and mud that are driven by their greater density relative to seawater. They are capable of flowing many miles down submarine canyons over very low slopes and transporting large volumes of sediment.

Millions of cubic yards are lost from California's beaches each year, and this is why the beaches do not get any wider. Ultimately, these former beach sands are deposited far offshore as deep-sea fans, much like an alluvial fan at the foot of a mountain range. With their final resting places at depths of 10,000 to 15,000 feet below sea level, these sands are, in effect, gone. Concerns over the losses of beach sand due to dams and reservoirs on our coastal streams have led to proposals to dam these offshore canyons as a way to trap this sand so that it can be pumped back onto the beaches. Dredging sand up from deep water would be a very expensive process, and it would be far easier and less expensive, and would consume less energy, to halt or trap the flow of sand at the shoreline before it moves offshore into a canyon head.

Disappearing Beaches:
Cutting Off the Sand

The development of California has had profound impacts on our shoreline. Hundreds of dams have been built on the state's rivers and coastal streams for water supply, flood control, or recreation. These are the same rivers that carry sand to our beaches, but the sand cannot get over or through most of these dams. Debris basins have been built throughout southern California to protect housing developments from mud or debris flows coming from the steep slopes of the San Bernardino, San Gabriel, and Santa Monica mountains. These basins trap coarse sediment such as sand and gravel while allowing the passage of water and fine sediment. Beginning in the mid-to-late 1800s, more than 1,400 dams over 25 feet high, or impounding more than 50 acre-feet of water, have been constructed throughout California, with over 500 of these dams located in the coastal watersheds that formerly drained directly to the shoreline (Figure 124). These barriers have reduced the supply of sand to the state's coastline by about 25 percent, and have now impounded about 200 million cubic yards of sand. That is 20 million dump truck loads of sand, or enough to build a beach 100 feet wide and 10 feet deep along nearly the entire length of California's 1,100-mile coastline! Although this was not an intended consequence of dam construction, it was a predictable outcome. The benefits of flood control or increased water supply and recreation have been countered to some degree by the gradual reduction of sand input to the shoreline from these dammed rivers, as well as the disruption of anadromous fish migration.

Some of the greatest impacts have occurred in southern California, where the demand for recreational beaches is largest. The sand load of the Ventura River has been reduced by about 50 percent, and that of the Los Angeles, San Gabriel, and Santa Ana rivers reduced about 67 percent by dams and debris basins. Although mining of the beaches and dunes no longer takes place, the construction and aggregate industries still remove sand and gravel in large volumes from seasonally dry streambeds and alluvial floodplains in southern California. In Los Angeles County alone, about 21 million cubic yards of sand and gravel are extracted from the

Figure 124. Locations of major dams on California's rivers and streams.

floodplains annually. Each cubic yard of sand extracted from a streambed or alluvial plain or fan represents a potential reduction in sand supply to the downstream beaches. There are also 115 debris basins in Los Angeles County alone that trap the coarse sediments coming out of the steep mountain drainages. Over 20 million cubic yards of material, much of it sand, have been removed from these basins and deposited in inland disposal sites, which also represents a significant reduction in sand delivery to the area's beaches.

The central and northern California sand supply has been considerably less altered. Major dams are few, and sand and gravel mining is more limited. The sand supply of the Klamath River has been reduced by 37 percent, the Russian River by 17 percent, the Salinas River by 33 percent, and the Carmel River by 59 percent due to dam construction. San Clemente Dam was constructed on a tributary to the Carmel River in 1921 and is now 90 percent filled with 2.5 million cubic yards of sediment (Figure 125).

Figure 125. The reservoir behind San Clemente Dam on the Carmel River is now about 90 percent full of sediment. Photo Gary Griggs.

Dumping sand on the beaches from a number of large coastal construction projects essentially kept pace with sediment losses from dam construction over much of the twentieth century. Several large marinas were dredged out of coastal wetlands (Marina del Rey and Oceanside Harbor, for example), and many large construction projects were undertaken in areas occupied by coastal dunes (the Hyperion Sewage Treatment Plant, the El Segundo Oil Refinery, and the Los Angeles International Airport, for example). Between 1940 and 1960, over 130 million cubic yards of sand were placed on the region's beaches from these large construction projects near the coast, so that the beaches remained wide and healthy.

By the late 1960s, however, these large dredging and construction projects and the associated beach nourishment activities were finished. In some areas, the nourishment projects built beaches that were broader than those previously maintained by natural sand supply. In other areas, nourishment from construction balanced the losses from dam building. Today, sand is no longer supplied from construction projects, but the sand impoundment behind the many dams continues. With the damaging El Niño Southern Oscillation (ENSO) events and severe storms of 1982–83, 1988, and 1997–98 and the apparent narrowing of some southern California beaches, there has been considerable discussion and several proposals put forward to remove dams that are filled with sediment and no longer serve any useful purpose. Although many dams impound large volumes of sediment and could be removed, two dams in particular—the Matilija Dam on the Ventura River and the Rindge Dam on Malibu Creek—have been targeted for study and ultimate removal.

Matilija Dam is located on Matilija Creek, a tributary to the Ventura River, about 18 miles inland from the coast. The dam is a concrete arch structure about 200 feet high built in

Figure 126. Matilija Dam on the Ventura River is now nearly filled with sediment and no longer serves any useful purpose. Photo A. Paul Jenkin.

1946 for water supply and flood control (Figure 126). When surveyed in 1999, however, the reservoir contained about six million cubic yards of sediment, and about 93 percent of the water storage capacity had been lost (Figure 127). Concerns about both the effects of sand supply reduction along the shoreline as well as the safety of the dam led to a proposal for removal. Although the dam could be taken down and sediment removed through incremental notching, the reliance on periodic high stream flows to transport the sediment to the coast has the potential to impact downstream properties, water intakes, and stream and estuary flora and fauna. On the other hand, dam removal could restore a remnant steelhead run in the Ventura River as well as provide needed beach sand.

Rindge Dam on Malibu Creek is about three miles inland from the coast. A private landowner, May Knight Rindge, who owned the Malibu Ranch at the time, built this 100-foot-high concrete structure in 1926 for private

Figure 127. This view of the upstream side of Matilija Dam shows some of the six million cubic yards of sediment that has accumulated in the reservoir. Photo A. Paul Jenkin.

water supply. By the late 1950s sediment had completely filled the reservoir, which now stores somewhere between 800,000 and 1.6 million cubic yards of sediment, about half of which is believed to be suitable for beach replenishment. Malibu Creek has historically been an important sediment source for the Malibu coastline. The California Department of Fish and Game, the U.S. Bureau of Reclamation, and the U.S. Army Corps of Engineers have all studied the feasibility of removing the dam. They concluded that there are shoreline benefits of dam removal and sediment delivery to the coast, but, as with the Matilija Dam or any other dam removal, potential downstream habitat impacts have yet to be resolved.

In July 2007, a blast of explosives cracked the face of Marmot Dam on the Sandy River in Oregon. This was a key step in the largest dam removal in the Pacific Northwest in 40 years, which was very thoroughly studied and monitored.

This dam was taken down to restore a salmon fishery. There were concerns about how long it would take to disperse the sand and gravel downstream and how this would affect the fish, however sediment moved much more rapidly than expected and Coho salmon were migrating upstream past the site within just three days of dam removal. These are encouraging results for the agencies considering dam removal in California.

Restoring and Nourishing Beaches

Almost all of us love the beach. In addition to recreational value, however, beaches also provide shoreline protection from storm waves and high tides, as well as important wildlife habitats. There are many areas along the coastline of California, however, where there are no beaches, or those that are present are naturally very narrow or have narrowed over time. In fact, long or continuous beaches front only about 28 percent, or 310 miles, of California's coast. Much of the high-relief mountainous coastline, such as the Mendocino and Big Sur coasts, much of the coast from Santa Cruz to San Francisco, and even much of the Santa Monica Mountains and northern San Diego coastlines have only small pocket beaches at the mouths of the coastal streams or very narrow beaches that disappear at high tide. The lack of an adequate supply of sand, a very steep intertidal zone such that a beach cannot form, the orientation of the shoreline relative to the angle of wave approach, or the lack of a suitable barrier to littoral transport, can all be reasons why there is no beach in some particular area.

Beaches not only change widths seasonally, but they can change over periods of several decades in response to cycles of climate change. During periods of intense or prolonged rainfall and high stream flow, for example, rivers transport large volumes of sand to the coast that widen the beaches. The opposite situation occurs during drier periods, and beaches may narrow in response.

In addition to these natural cycles or fluctuations in beach width, human have also significantly impacted California's beaches. The coastline from Santa Barbara to San Diego has been altered by a number of large coastal engineering structures, primarily jetties and breakwaters.

The Santa Cruz and Santa Barbara small craft harbors are good examples of these large-scale coastline modifications and ones that have had significant shoreline impacts. Castle or Seabright Beach in Santa Cruz is a good example. Prior to the construction of the jetties at the entrance to the Santa Cruz Harbor in 1963, there was no winter beach as the storm waves pounded the bluffs at high tide (Figure 128). Erosion of the bluffs threatened and destroyed structures and the roadway. Even in the summer months the beach was relatively narrow and only provided limited recreational area

Figure 128. The Castle on Seabright Beach at high tide during a storm in 1953. Photo Courtesy of Santa Cruz Natural History Museum.

Figure 129. Seabright Beach around the 1950s, prior to the construction of Santa Cruz Small Craft Harbor.

(Figure 129). With the completion of the jetties, hundreds of thousands of cubic yards of sand accumulated behind the upcoast jetty, and a half-mile-long beach formed that gradually increased in width to about 400 feet (Figure 130). The

Figure 130. Seabright Beach in 2006. Photo Gary Griggs.

Figure 131. A large area of sand accumulated upcoast of the breakwater at Santa Barbara following its construction in 1930 and is now covered with a park, road, parking lot, and sports stadium for Santa Barbara City College. Photo Bruce Perry, CSULB Geological Sciences.

summer beach provided a greatly expanded recreational area, which also buffered the formerly eroding bluffs from wave attack. The already narrow beaches downcoast from the harbor eroded, however, and extensive shoreline armoring soon followed the increased bluff erosion. A very similar story unfolded following construction of the Santa Barbara Harbor about 35 years earlier. A large beach accumulated upcoast (Figure 131), and sand losses and erosion occurred for miles downcoast, ultimately leading to the collapse of houses built on the back-beach at Carpentaria.

In both cases, as well as at the sites of many other large coastal engineering projects, dredging has been the solution. Sand is regularly pumped from harbor entrances to the downcoast beaches at considerable annual cost in order to restore littoral transport of sand and to allow the downcoast beaches to recover. This has been called beach restoration or nourishment, but it is really just sand bypassing. We're just moving the sand from one side of the harbor to the other in order to keep the flow of sand moving along the shoreline.

Beach nourishment or beach restoration is the placement of sand on the shoreline to widen beaches that are naturally narrow or where the supply of sand has been significantly reduced through natural processes or human disturbances. Between 1930 and 1993 over 130 million cubic yards of sand was added to the beaches of southern California in various nourishment projects. About half of this volume was split between the beaches of Santa Monica Bay and the area between Coronado and the Mexican border. The beaches widened significantly as a result and remained wide for many years. This sand, and most of the sand added artificially to the beaches of California historically, was a by-product of large coastal construction or maintenance projects where very large volumes of sand became available. As new marinas were constructed or flood control channels cleared, this sand was also added to the beaches in a process called opportunistic beach nourishment. In other words, the sand was a by-product of a construction or maintenance project, so the beach was a convenient place to dispose of the extra sand.

In addition to opportunistic beach nourishment, there are other projects where sand has been added to the beach for the sole purpose of either widening an existing beach or attempting to build one where it previously did not exist (Figures 132 and 133). Sand may come from either offshore sources or onshore sources (dunes, river channels, or sand quarries, for example). Depending upon the source, the method of excavation and transport, as well as the transport distance involved, nourishment costs can vary considerably. The major concerns with any nourishment project are how much it will cost, who bears the cost, and how long the sand will last. Although beach nourishment may initially sound like a good solution for widening beaches and providing more recreational area, as well as increasing protection of the

Figure 132. The SANDAG beach nourishment project in 2001 dredged 2 million cubic yards of sand from offshore and placed it on 12 San Diego County beaches at a total cost of $17.5 million. Pictured is the Batiquitos Beach portion of the nourishment project. Photo James Dickens, Great Lakes Dredge and Dock.

Figure 133. Sand dredged from offshore and placed on the beach at Oceanside as part of the 2001 SANDAG beach nourishment project is being spread out along the beach by a bulldozer. Photo James Dickens, Great Lakes Dredge and Dock.

backshore area, there may be many reasons why there is no beach or a narrow beach in a particular area. It is unrealistic to expect sand added artificially to a stretch of shoreline to remain when no sand accumulated there naturally, regardless of how much was spent and how well intentioned our efforts.

What You Should Remember about Beaches

There are some important things you should remember about beaches. (1) Beaches provide important recreational areas for residents and visitors alike, as well as biological habitats, (2) they provide a buffer to the backshore and coastline to wave attack, (3) they may be ephemeral and undergo regular and sometimes dramatic seasonal changes, and (4) many human activities can affect beaches.

As a dynamic and fragile feature, a beach may grow, shrink, alter its shape, or even disappear in a single storm. During winter, large, steep, closely spaced waves scour away beach sand and move it offshore. When the weather calms in spring, waves that are less steep and more widely spaced normally push the sand back onshore and rebuild the wide summer beach. This is a natural seasonal process by which the beach strategically adapts to high winter storm waves and low summer swell. Remember that the beach and the ocean are in a dynamic equilibrium, so that when one changes, the other must adjust. So if a house is built on a wide beach during summer, it should be no surprise for the owner to discover the ocean in the living room during a winter storm. In addition to the seasonal onshore and offshore movement of sand, large volumes of beach sand move alongshore in most locations, driven by waves approaching the shoreline at an angle.

The development of California has been accompanied by large-scale changes to the landscape and major alterations or disruptions to natural systems. Dams and debris basins have been built, rivers and creeks have been paved or concreted over, sand has been quarried for construction, and harbors and other large coastal engineering structures have been built along the shoreline. Each of these actions has altered the natural flow of sand to or along the state's beaches, particularly in central and southern California, where the recreational demand on beaches is greatest. Although there are no simple solutions, we now recognize the problems and disruptions we have created and have begun to evaluate various responses and solutions. The approaches we develop today need to be sustainable and to rely as much as possible on natural processes.

Our Underwater Edge: The Continental Shelf

Geologically speaking, the shoreline we drive, bike, or walk along today is only a temporary feature. As sea level has risen and fallen repeatedly over the last several million years, the position of the shoreline has moved back and forth across the edge of the continent in response (Figure 8). When the global climate is colder, water evaporates from the oceans and accumulates as snow and ice on the continents, expanding the glaciers and continental ice sheets. Sea level drops in response, and when this happens the shoreline moves westward and leaves a beach and tide pools behind. When the climate is warmer, as it is today, glaciers and ice sheets melt and retreat, which increases the volume of water in the oceans, and the coastline moves landward again.

Warmer and cooler periods, which drive the rise and fall of sea level, occur about every 20,000 years or so, and the flooded edge of California has experienced this process many, many times. As the shoreline repeatedly moved landward and seaward, wave action eroded and tended to smooth out the underwater topography, just as the winter waves erode and smooth the intertidal and near shore seafloor today.

The result of this constant back and forth migration of the shoreline and the associated wave erosion of the seafloor has been the formation of a relatively flat continental shelf along the state's entire coast. The continental shelf is essentially the flooded edge of California. It starts at the shoreline and extends offshore to average depths of 350 to 400 feet, where the seafloor steepens from less than 1 degree across the shelf to 5 degrees or more as it descends to the deep sea floor some 10,000 feet below (Figure 134). The shelf varies considerably in width from very narrow, a mile or two, off the Big Sur coast, to 35 miles off the Golden Gate, but more typically ranging from about five to 15 miles. The depth to

Figure 134. A topographic relief map of Southern California including the offshore seafloor showing the nearly flat continental shelf, the more steeply sloping continental slope, and the many submarine canyons cutting across both features. Image United States Geological Survey.

the outer edge of the shelf, 350 to 400 feet, is approximately the maximum level to which sea level has fall over the past million or so years.

The continental shelf overall is relatively flat and feature-less as a result of the bedrock abrasion by waves for thousands of years, but also due to the deposition of sediments derived from land, which have filled in the depressions and mantled the rocks over the eons (Figure 134). The shelf is not com-pletely smooth, there are rock outcrops, depressions, and a few islands, but overall it is a relatively flat feature. Although there are some major differences between the underlying geology of the oceans basins and that of the continents, the geologic formations or rock types underlying the shelf are similar to, and extensions of, the rocks exposed on the adja-cent coastline. We know this from imaging and sampling the continental shelf and from the rocks exposed on the offshore islands.

Grand Canyons on the Seafloor

The presence of canyons on the seafloor, similar to those on land, came as a surprise to early oceanographers who first noticed them incised into the continental shelf and slope off of the mid-Atlantic coast over a century ago. As active exploration of California's coastal waters and offshore area began in the early 1900s, a number of submarine canyons were soon also discovered here. Those immediately offshore of the Scripps Institution of Oceanography at La Jolla, appropriately named Scripps Canyon and La Jolla Canyon, were among the first charted and studied in detail, and before long canyons were discovered along almost the entire length of California's continental shelf and slope. Marine geologists depended for years solely on the two-dimensional records produced by fathometers or depth recorders until the development of multi-beam technology, so it was only the most prominent seafloor canyons that were initially recognized. Over the past decade, however, with digital technology and 3-D imaging, many more submarine canyons have been recognized and surveyed, such as those cutting into the continental shelf and slope between Santa Barbara and Point Conception (Figure 135).

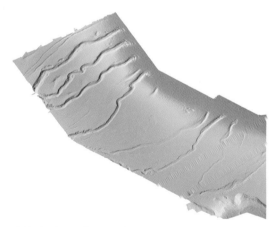

Figure 135. Seafloor topography east of Point Conception showing the Arguello submarine canyons that have been eroded into the continental shelf and slope. Image © 1996 Monterey Bay Aquarium Research Institute.

Most of the largest submarine canyons were given names, usually based on their proximity to some nearby terrestrial feature or community, so we ended up with Coronado Canyon, Newport Canyon, San Pedro Canyon, Redondo Canyon, Santa Monica Canyon (Figure 134), Dume Canyon, Mugu Canyon, and Hueneme Canyon along the southern California coast. Carmel Canyon and Monterey Canyon are the most prominent submarine canyons along the central coast (Figure 136), although there are others as well. Farther north, Mattole Canyon, Mendocino Canyon, and Eel Canyon are among the largest.

Submarine canyons are similar in many ways to river canyons or drainage systems on land. They are dominantly erosional features that are carved into the continental shelf and slope, often exposing bedrock in the canyon walls. They typically have windy or sinuous courses and may have a number of tributaries or branching channels, especially in their

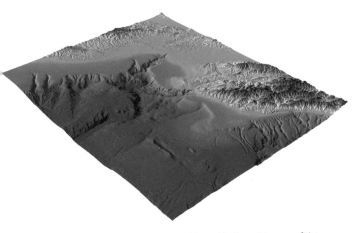

Figure 136. Three-dimensional topographic and bathymetric map of the Monterey Bay area showing the Santa Lucia Range along the Big Sur coast and also the offshore submarine canyons as well as Monterey and Carmel submarine canyons. Image United States Geological Survey.

inner reaches (Figure 136). All submarine canyons extend from the outer edge of the continental shelf, down the continental slope to the deep seafloor. While some of California's canyons extend no closer to shore than the edge of the shelf, others extend completely across the shelf nearly to the beach. Most of the prominent southern California canyons, as well as Carmel and Monterey canyons, extend into shallow water near river mouths, which gives us some clues as to the origins of these interesting seafloor features.

Following the initial discovery of submarine canyons off the Atlantic coast of the United States, and for many years thereafter, there were two competing views on the origins of these mysterious seafloor features. Because they seemed to resemble river valleys or canyons on land, and also because many of the submarine canyons first surveyed were located directly offshore from river mouths, some geologists believed that these submarine canyons must have been eroded by the adjacent rivers when sea level was lower during past Ice Ages. It was known that the continental shelves were exposed during those glacial periods, so the belief was that these rivers simply continued cutting their channels across the now-exposed seafloor. This was not a problem for the sections of the canyons that crossed the continental shelf, which only extended to depths of 350 to 400 feet, but presented some major difficulties for the portions that extended down the continental slope to the deep seafloor, some 10,000 to 12,000 feet or more deeper. Relying on rivers to cut the canyons to depths of 10,000 feet or more would have required draining most of the water from the world's oceans. Over time, however, the advocates for the subaerial, or river erosion hypothesis for submarine canyons realized that emptying the oceans simply was not geologically possible. There just was not any place to put that huge volume of water.

The alternative view was that underwater processes had cut the canyons, or that they had a submarine origin. The major shortcoming with this hypothesis was that there was not any process that had been observed 50 or 60 years ago that seemed capable of cutting canyons hundreds of feet deep on the seafloor, and in the case of portions of Monterey and Carmel canyons, apparently through granite. Several subsequent discoveries, however, began to help answer the question of how all this could have happened underwater.

Layers of sand were discovered in the first sediment cores that were recovered from the floors of submarine canyons. For years marine geologists have dropped corers, which are long steel pipes with heavy weights attached, into the seafloor from ships to extract cores of the sediments. The sediment layers provide a history book or record of what processes have taken place over time at that particular location on the seafloor. When the sand layers from submarine canyons were analyzed carefully, we recognized that they were graded, or the sand was coarsest at the bottom and finest at the top. This graded bedding can be created in a jar of mixed sediment (gravel, sand, silt, and clay, for example) and water if we shake it up and let the sediments settle out. The gravel settles fastest and ends up at the bottom of the jar, followed by the coarsest sand, then finer sand, and finally silt, and hours later, the clay. So the graded sediment recovered from the floors of a number of different submarine canyons indicated that these sediments had settled out of suspension. Additionally, even though many of these sediments were recovered from depths of hundreds or thousands of feet below sea level, they contained shallow water fossils, indicating that the sediments came from shallow water. The concept that emerged from these observations was that underwater flows of muddy and sandy sediments, which were given the name turbidity currents, could be generated in shallow water at the heads of these submarine canyons, perhaps from earthquakes, large storm waves, or river floods. These underwater avalanches would flow down slope along the seafloor, driven by gravity because the muddy sediments were denser than seawater. Sand is abrasive, which is why we use sandpaper to smooth

Figure 137. Turbidites in the Franciscan Formation exposed in a road cut near Devil's Slide, San Mateo County. Photo Deepika Shrestha Ross.

wood, and would enable these turbidity currents to progressively cut canyons across the continental shelf and slope over hundreds and thousands of years. Geologists working on land have recognized these turbidity current deposits, or turbidites, exposed in outcrops of old seafloor deposits all over the world (Figure 137).

A second fortuitous event provided the evidence needed to confirm the existence and, ultimately, the importance of underwater turbidity currents to submarine canyon formation. In 1929 there was a large earthquake off Nova Scotia in the Grand Banks area. At the time of that earthquake, we had no cell phones or orbiting satellites to relay phone calls, so a number of underwater cables had been laid along the seafloor to connect phone lines in North America with Europe. In the minutes and hours immediately following the earthquake, there was a well-documented cut-off in communications as these cables progressively failed proceeding down slope farther from the earthquake's epicenter. It appeared to the scientists who studied these cable failures that a submarine flow of sediments, or turbidity current, had been generated by the earthquake. As this large mass of sediment moved rapidly down slope, driven by gravity, it sequentially broke the telephone cables as it continued on its path to the deep seafloor. The confirming evidence was obtained when oceanographic vessels subsequently cored the sea floor in the area and found graded sands at the surface as evidence of the passage of the turbidity current.

Putting together all these observations, as well as many others, has produced a reasonably straightforward and coherent picture of how the submarine canyons off the California coast and elsewhere have formed. It turns out that both subaerial and submarine processes are involved. We need to have at least a portion of the continental shelf exposed to initiate the cutting of a submarine canyon. This happens at a location where a river discharges at the shoreline. As sea level drops during a cool or glacial period, the shoreline retreats across the shelf and the river will continue to erode its valley or channel across the continental shelf in order to reach the ocean. At least half of all the submarine canyons recognized globally lie directly offshore from rivers, which provides good evidence for the role of rivers in the initial formation of many submarine canyons.

With each rise in sea level, the river will retreat back across the shelf, where it will discharge at the new shoreline location. Some of the offshore canyons may fill or partially fill with seafloor sediments during these times of higher sea level. With the next drop in sea level, the river will again work its way across the shelf, removing or eroding any sediment that has accumulated in the offshore portion of the channel and further deepening it. The river's sediment load will now be discharged at the outer edge of the continental shelf, where it will accumulate until is becomes unstable, and then, either from an earthquake, large storm waves, or some other mechanism, the sediment will cascade down the steeper continental slope as a turbidity current. The abrasion by the coarser sand and gravel will gradually erode a canyon down the continental slope, while the finer-grained suspended silt and clay may be deposited along the banks of the canyon as natural levees, similar to a river in flood stage. Thus a submarine canyon can grow by both eroding its channel downward and constructing natural levees upward.

An essential process maintaining those submarine canyons along the California coast that cross the shelf and extend almost to the shoreline (Monterey and Carmel canyons, Mugu and Hueneme canyons, Redondo, Newport, and Scripps canyons, for example; Figures 135 and 136) is the active transport of littoral sand from the beaches into the canyon heads. As described in Chapter Five, most of California's littoral cells or beach compartments terminate in submarine canyons, with those between Point Conception and San Diego among the best understood. As waves from the northwest drive littoral drift southward, the sand at the end of the Santa Barbara, Zuma, Santa Monica, San Pedro, and Oceanside cells is transported offshore into the heads of the submarine canyons at the end of each cell (Figure 120). Hundreds of thousands of cubic yards of sand is funneled down into each of these canyon heads each year, to ultimately be carried by turbidity currents down to the deep seafloor 10,000 to 12,000 feet below. This abrasive sand continues the erosion or downcutting of these submarine canyons, and the canyons maintain their roles in the process of moving sand from the beaches to the deep sea.

Seeing through the Water: Imaging the Seafloor Offshore

Until fairly recently, marine geologists and others who studied the continental shelf had to be content using relatively simple fathometers or depth recorders to determine the depth at various locations using a single beam of sound. The continuous records of the seafloor collected just offshore did enable

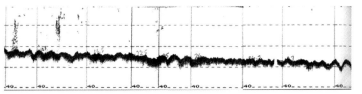

Figure 138. A fathometer record of a portion of the continental shelf of northern Santa Cruz County.

us to determine the depth and delineate those areas where the seafloor was smooth and sediment covered, or rough and irregular where rock was exposed (Figure 138). But the two-dimensional images had their limitations and gave us only a very limited view of the offshore seafloor topography immediately beneath the ship. This was like driving down the Pacific Coast Highway with blinders on so that all you could see was the landscape 20 feet on either side of the highway.

Technology has advanced significantly, however, so that we can now collect three-dimensional images of the seafloor using multi-beam bathymetry, which can cover a wide swath of seafloor with a single ship track. The new images, especially when color-coded by depth, have given us essentially a complete picture of the continental shelf with all of its detailed morphology. These records have revealed for the first time some astonishing features that were essentially hidden from our eyes (Figure 136). Scientists and non-scientists have a completely new appreciation for the complexities of the nearshore seafloor in areas that were always of interest, but for which we lacked a method of visual exploration.

Flooded Real Estate: The Seafloor off Los Angeles

The seafloor off of southern California (Figure 134), for example, has always been an area of interest and exploration, but now we can see the flat and relatively smooth continental shelf, the sharp break in slope down to the offshore basins, and the many submarine canyons that cut across the shelf and then make their way down the continental slope. These maps have been helpful in understanding how sediment moves from the shoreline through the canyons to the deep sea, which areas of the shelf are exposed rock and which are covered with sediment, and how the seafloor topography serves to refract incoming waves, thereby affecting how wave energy is concentrated or dispersed at the shoreline. The narrow shelf off of the steep Santa Monica Mountains on the left side of the image contrasts sharply with the much wider shelf that can be seen as an extension of the low-relief Los Angeles Basin on either side of the Palos Verdes peninsula.

Canyons and Landslides: The Santa Barbara Channel

Moving to the northwest, an image from the Santa Barbara coast (Figure 139) provides some of the most vivid examples ever seen of slope failure, or large landslides, along the steeper slopes of the Santa Barbara Channel. These are very similar to some of the earth flows seen in the hills surrounding the San Francisco Bay Area, which form after heavy and prolonged winter rains, but those in the Santa Barbara Channel are underwater. One probable cause of failures of this scale on the seafloor is large earthquakes, which we know are relatively frequent events throughout the southern California area. Although there was speculation that such events took place along these steeper offshore slopes, the multi-beam records proved their existence as well as their large size.

Farther west (Figure 135), several parallel submarine canyons have been documented, cutting into the outer edge of the continental shelf and then proceeding in a parallel fashion down the steeper continental slope to the deep seafloor. The canyons, while flowing at right angles to the coastline, do have meanders or bends along their courses, much like

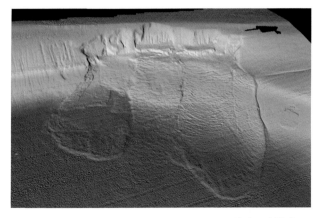

Figure 139. This colored bathymetric map shows the "Goleta Slide," a very large underwater landslide just west of Santa Barbara. Different sections of the slide may have failed at different times. The image was compiled by the Monterey Bay Aquarium Research Institute. Gary Greene © 1996 MBARI.

some rivers on land, and in some cases they merge, as do tributaries in terrestrial rivers.

Where the Mountains Meet the Sea: Big Sur and Monterey Bay

The Big Sur coastline and adjacent offshore area (Figure 136) is rugged and characterized by steep coastal mountains dropping abruptly to the coastline, and a very narrow continental shelf. Like the Santa Barbara Channel to the south, many submarine canyons notch the outer edge of the shelf and then extend for miles down the continental slope. Farther north, the shelf widens, and the low-relief topography surrounding Monterey Bay, like the Los Angeles basin, is mirrored in the offshore shelf, which is wide and relatively smooth (Figure 136). The Carmel River valley, which trends inland immediately south of the Monterey Peninsula,

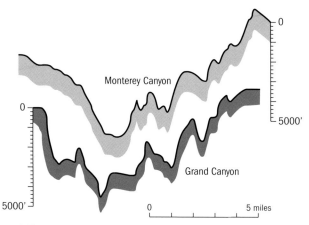

Figure 140. Profiles showing comparisons of relief of the Monterey Submarine Canyon and the Grand Canyon of the Colorado River.

terminates in Carmel Submarine Canyon, which slices into the shelf and then trends to the northwest to join the massive Monterey Submarine Canyon. Monterey Canyon is the largest submarine canyon along the west coast of North America and one of the deepest in the world, and is of comparable relief (over 5,000 feet) to the Grand Canyon of the Colorado River (Figure 140). The canyon extends from the shoreline at Moss Landing in the middle of Monterey Bay for almost 300 miles to depths of over 12,000 feet. Years of study of the onshore geology provide evidence that the entire drainage of California's vast Central Valley formerly drained through this area, rather than through the Golden Gate to the north. Millions of years of discharge of water and sediment from this huge inland drainage system provided the erosional mechanism needed to carve the inner portion of this large submarine canyon when sea level was lower. Turbidity currents were responsible for creating the deeper portions of this and California's other offshore canyons.

Below Mavericks

The word "Mavericks" has joined the list of that handful of places scattered around the globe where unique seafloor topography produces huge waves under the right conditions. These waves went unknown and unsurfed for decades; they were finally discovered, surfed secretly for a number of years, and then became an overnight legend. California's big wave surfing spot owes its towering 40- to 50-foot waves to a bedrock ledge on the seafloor just north of Half Moon Bay where water depths decrease from about 70 feet to 20 feet over a very short distance (Figure 103). Waves lurch upward quickly as they are compressed into shallower water and also refract or wrap around the bulge, creating a bowl where waves reach greater heights than at any other place along California's coastline. When Mavericks goes off each year under the right storm and wave conditions, a select group of big wave surfers from around the world are invited to an annual contest.

Under the Golden Gate

The first reported discovery of San Francisco Bay by a European was in November 1769 by the Spaniard Gaspar de Portola, who was traveling by land. He was unable to recognize Monterey Bay and so continued north, where he ultimately saw San Francisco Bay from the hills where Hwy. 280 passes above the San Francisco airport. Six years later, on August 5, 1775, another Spanish explorer, Juan de Ayala, sailed his ship, the San Carlos, through the Golden Gate and anchored near Angel Island. In 1937 the Golden Gate Bridge was completed across this 1.7-mile-wide entrance to one of the world's greatest natural harbors (Figure 141). The bridge was the largest single span suspension bridge ever built at the time of its construction.

The bay itself has gone through some enormous changes from the mid-1800s onward as mining for gold in the upstream watersheds, the dumping of debris, and artificial fill

Figure 141. The Golden Gate Bridge and San Francisco Bay. Photo Kenneth and Gabrielle Adelman, California Coastal Records Project, www.CaliforniaCoastline.org.

for construction all served to decrease the size and depth of the bay. Large-scale hydraulic mining during the California Gold Rush released staggering amounts of sediment from the upstream rivers, which was transported downstream. One respected estimate of the amount of total debris carried downstream totals more than eight times the amount of rock and earth removed during the construction of the Panama Canal. The eroded material was carried downstream until it reached the still waters of the bay where it settled out, eventually filling in large parts of Suisun, San Pablo, and San Francisco bays.

The subsequent growth and development of San Francisco, Oakland, Berkeley, and the other cities around the margins of the bay forever changed the shoreline as dune sand, building debris, and old ship hulls were used to extend the bay margins outward so more construction could take place. Ultimately, about one-third of the entire bay was filled as marshes, wetlands, and the shallow tidal flats became waste disposal sites, airports, port facilities, highways, housing developments, and even a baseball stadium (Figure 142). Several factors made the bay particularly susceptible to being

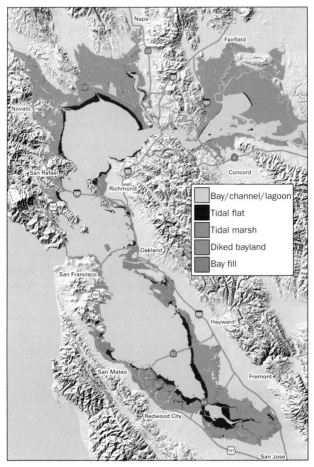

Figure 142. The changing outline of San Francisco Bay due to filling around the margins. Image courtesy of the San Francisco Estuary Institute.

filled: (1) much of the bay is very shallow, with about two-thirds less than 18 feet deep; (2) much of the shoreline of the bay has been in private ownership; (3) many different federal, state, and local government agencies have control over different sections of the bay shoreline; and (4) filling had a long history and was thought for decades to be a beneficial activity.

Concern over the continuing filling of the bay and the effects on the water quality, wildlife habitat, and other amenities led to the formation of the Bay Conservation and Development Commission (BCDC) in 1965, which began to bring the filling of the bay under control. Dredging, however, to open up and maintain shipping channels, as well as the dredging of sand from the floor of the bay by mining concessions, continues to modify the floor of the bay. Images of the floor of San Francisco Bay reveal rocky outcrops, smooth sediment-covered areas, and large sand waves or current ripples approaching the Golden Gate (Figure 143). As bottom-current velocities increase with each flood and ebb tide, they begin to move the sand on the seabed, and if the water is moving fast enough, dunes or ripples begin to form and migrate in the direction of the current.

High-resolution multi-beam imaging of the seafloor immediately outside of the Golden Gate by the U.S. Geological Survey (USGS) and university scientists in 2004

Figure 143. A portion of the seafloor of San Francisco Bay showing large ripples and other seafloor features. Image United States Geological Survey.

Figure 144. A seafloor image off of the Golden Gate showing some of the largest underwater sand waves discovered anywhere in the world. Image Patrick Barnard, United States Geological Survey.

and 2005 produced some astounding results. A series of huge sand waves with heights of over 30 feet and with distances between crests of over 700 feet were discovered in water depths of 300 feet (Figure 144). These large sand waves are the result of the over 500 billion gallons of water that are forced through the narrow Golden Gate every six hours during each tidal cycle. The resulting very strong tidal currents, well known to mariners who enter and exit the bay, sweep the sediments through the channel and then distribute them on the seafloor just outside the Golden Gate where they have formed one of the largest fields of sand waves in the world. These impressive sea floor sand waves essentially had their origins in the foothills of the Sierra Nevada during the California Gold Rush 160 years ago when sand was hydraulically washed by the '49ers from the hillsides into the creeks and rivers to start its long course downstream to the bay and finally the ocean.

Resources of the Continental Shelf

Offshore Energy

The seafloor as well as the waters overlying California's continental shelf are major contributors to California's economy. By far the largest component of these offshore resources is the oil and gas industry. About 25 to 30 percent of the 85 million barrels of oil used globally each day is pumped from offshore, primarily from the relatively shallow waters of the continental shelf off many different countries.

In California, the first oil wells drilled near the coastline were at Signal Hill near Long Beach and in the Ventura basin to the north. Petroleum geologists soon realized, however, that the same oil-bearing reservoirs that were being drilled on land also extended offshore beneath the continental shelf. Slant drilling, also known as whip-stocking, in which rigs on land angle their drill bits offshore, was followed by drilling from piers. California was home to the first U.S. offshore oil production when a wooden pier was built at Summerland, just south of Santa Barbara, in 1896. Twenty-two companies constructed 14 different piers, and just after the turn of the century there were over 400 offshore wells (Figure 145). This

Figure 145. Oil piers and wells off Summerland, Santa Barbara County, in the early 1900s. Photo United States Geological Survey.

Figure 146. A pier leading to an artificial island (Rincon Island) for oil drilling and production off Punda Gorda, Ventura County. Photo Bruce Perry, CSULB Geological Sciences.

first offshore drilling adventure lasted about 25 years, and by about 1920 only a few of the wells were still active.

Piers were limited in how far they could extend offshore, however, so the next step was a pier extended offshore to an artificial island (Figure 146), which extended the drilling capability a little farther offshore. Realizing the limitations of this approach, the petroleum industry began the construction of progressively larger and more expensive platforms for offshore drilling, many of these visible driving along the Santa Barbara and Ventura coastlines today (Figure 147). Federal oil and gas leases offshore southern California today support 23 different platforms and 1,500 active wells, which produce about 26 million barrels of oil annually. At $40/barrel, this amounts to a little over a billion dollars annually. In 2008 the revenues from federal offshore leases to California was $250 million. The United States uses about 22 million barrels each day, so the platforms off of California provide only about 28 hours, or a little over a day, of our annual oil usage. Those wells in federal waters, or beyond

Figure 147. Offshore oil platforms in the Santa Barbara Channel.

the three-mile state limit, have produced a total of more than one billion barrels of oil.

Natural seepage of petroleum, both from the seafloor off the coast of Santa Barbara and along the shoreline itself, has been known for over 450 years. Juan Rodriguez Cabrillo first recorded these seeps in 1542, and he and his crew used the tar or asphaltum to caulk two of his ships, just as the native Chumash had done for centuries with their canoes. English explorer George Vancouver, during his trip up the Pacific Coast in 1792, noted in his journals that the Santa Barbara Channel was covered in all directions with an oily surface. Offshore surveys indicate that there may be as many as 2,000 active seafloor oil seeps that release about 10,000 gallons of oil every day.

Forty years ago, a major oil spill took place beneath Platform A in the Santa Barbara Channel when a blowout occurred during the drilling process. Oil boiled up into the water for 11 days before the well and adjacent seafloor could be sealed with grout. About 3.4 million gallons of oil were spilled, spreading across 800 square miles of ocean and scarring 35 miles of shoreline. This was a wake-up call and spurred the establishment of the National Environmental Protection Agency (NEPA) and the Clean Air Act in 1970, as well as stronger federal regulation of the oil industry. Since the Santa Barbara spill, offshore drilling has only spilled a reported 852 barrels of oil as a result of better technology and regulatory vigilance. This single event, however, left an impression on most Californians of the hazards and potential problems of offshore drilling that still persists 40 years later. A major debate rages today about whether the oil companies should be required to remove the platforms completely when their productivity declines to unprofitable levels, or whether they should be allowed to leave them in place after removing the abovewater portions to a safe depth for ship traffic. This process, referred to as "rigs to reefs," is very contentious and pits the oil industry and some recreational fishermen, who believe that there are local benefits for fishing, against many environmental organizations and the commercial fishermen who want the platforms removed completely.

Living Marine Resources

The waters overlying the continental shelf, particularly those along the eastern boundaries of the ocean basins such as California, are among the most productive on Earth. The primary reason for this high biological productivity is due to the process of upwelling, which normally occurs each spring and early summer. Winds from the northwest dominate along the California coast at this time of year, which drive the offshore California Current southward. The surface waters of the ocean, however, are also influenced by Earth's rotation. This process, known as the Coriolis effect, causes surface currents in the Northern Hemisphere to be deflected 90 degrees to the right of their direction of movement. As a result, the surface waters tend to move offshore and are replaced by bottom waters that rise to the surface,

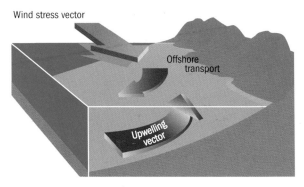

Figure 148. Upwelling brings cold, nutrient- rich water to the surface in the spring and early summer along the California coast. Image Wendelin Montciel.

a process called upwelling (Figure 148). This deeper water is typically rich in nutrients from the decomposing organic matter, which is constantly sinking to the bottom. The combination of the nutrients, which serve as fertilizer, and the exposure to the longer days and sunlight of spring and summer, lead to blooms in the phytoplankton, which are the small floating algae. These microscopic plants, such as diatoms (Figure 149), in turn are fed on by the zooplankton, or the small floating animals such as krill (Figure 150). The

Figure 149. Photomicrograph of a diatom.

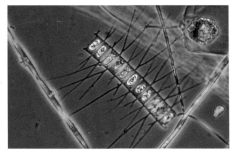

Figure 150. Krill, an important food source for many marine organisms from sardines to whales. Photo Dr. Ted Gaten, University of Leicester, UK.

growth of the small plants and animals serve as the base of the food chain that provides the food for all those marine animals higher up the food chain, the fish and shellfish, sea lions and whales, for example.

Globally, upwelling regions only constitute about 0.1 percent of the surface area of the oceans, but are the areas where about 95 percent of the annual global production of marine biomass occurs and account for about 21 percent of the world's fishery landings. The fertile waters offshore California have been fished for as long as there have been humans occupying the coast. Native Americans stayed close to shore, fishing in the bays, estuaries, and tide pools, but the Chinese, Japanese, Italians, Azoreans, Portuguese, and others all discovered different resources they could harvest from the waters over the continental shelf. At different times over the past 150 years these included abalone, sea urchins, crabs, prawns, squid, sardines, anchovies, rockfish, salmon, sea otters, whales, and just about everything else that had any value to humans.

For a variety of reasons, however, many fisheries that flourished for years and supported entire industries and cultures have now been relegated to the history books. Each fishery or resource has its own history and reasons for decline, although often it was a simple matter of overfishing, taking out more of the resource than could be sustained. In 2006, the most recent year for which complete data are available, California's fishing ports reported a total catch value of just over $130 million from 167,000 tons of commercial fish and other living marine species. For historic contrast, this is less than one-fourth of the yearly tonnage of sardines alone landed during the peak of the sardine industry in the 1930s and 1940s.

The California market squid is an example of one fishery that is still doing well. It is California's largest fishery by tonnage (Table 3) and is the second highest in terms of total value at nearly $27 million in 2006. In large part this is due to the squid having a one-year life cycle, so a new generation comes along every year. In contrast, many of the rockfish

TABLE 3 California Dept. of Fish and Game 2006 Catch Statistics

Fish/Shellfish	Total Tons	Value
Anchovy	14,100 (4)	$1,300,000
Bonito	2,740 (9)	$1,530,000
Calif. Halibut	358	$2,712,000
Pacific Mackerel	7,790 (5)	$1,016,000
Rockfish	645	$2,260,000
Sablefish	1,779 (10)	$4,890,000 (7)
Chinook Salmon	516	$5,255,000 (4)
Pacific Sardine	51,341 (2)	$5,088,000 (6)
Sole	3,293 (8)	$3,546,000 (9)
Swordfish	410	$2,719,000
Thornyhead	981	$2,355,000
Pacific Whiting	5,984 (6)	$1,360,000
Dungeness Crab	13,085 (3)	$44,869,000 (1)
Calif. Spiny Lobster	443	$8,058,000 (3)
Prawns	241	$3,821,000 (8)
Red Urchin	5,330 (7)	$5,141,000 (5)
Market Squid	54,182 (1)	$26,940,000 (2)
Totals	167,088 tons	$130,273,000

Note: Number in parentheses indicates ranking in tonnage and value.

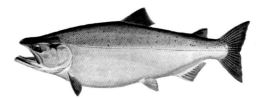

Figure 151. A Chinook salmon.

live for decades and don't reproduce until they are eight or 10 years old. We have overfished many of these populations such that they are down to a fraction of their original numbers, and the sizes of the catches, as well as the sizes of the fish, have declined year after year. The total value of all rockfish harvested commercially in 2006 was only $2.2 million, the price of a single coastal home in some California communities.

The salmon fishery is a slightly different story (Figure 151). The commercial salmon fishery was severely restricted by the federal government in 2006 and completely closed in 2008 and 2009 because the populations had dropped to such low numbers. Two decades ago there were over 10,000 permitted commercial salmon boats, whereas today there are only about 1,000. Salmon are anadromous, spawning in fresh water but then swimming downstream to the ocean where they spend most of their lives. When mature after two to four years, they return to the streams where they were born to complete the cycle and spawn again. Salmon require clean sand and gravel for their spawning as well as adequate river flows. The gradual decline in the salmon population and the loss of most of the commercial fishery is complex, but biologists believe that it is due to a combination of human-caused and natural factors, including both marine and freshwater conditions such as dams and water diversions, siltation and habitat alterations, as well as pollution. In the offshore ocean, changing ocean temperatures and greatly reduced upwelling in recent years appear to have seriously affected the availability of food for salmon.

The Monterey Bay sardine fishery was a product of the upwelling phenomena described earlier and was immortalized by John Steinbeck in *Cannery Row*. The right combination of light, nutrients, plankton, and the fact that sardines are filter feeders that eat plankton directly, all combined to form the foundation for a sardine industry along the west coast that stretched from Southern California to British Columbia. The fishery flourished from the mid-1920s to about 1950, and for a while California's sardine fishery became the largest in the Western Hemisphere, with 726,000 tons of sardines landed in California in 1937. Again, for historical contrast, in 2006 the California rockfish catch totaled 645 tons and the catch of Chinook salmon was 516 tons.

Since the late 1920s, the culture and economy of Monterey's Cannery Row had developed around the sardines, as Monterey became the heart and soul of the sardine fishery (Figure 152). From 1945 onward, however, the population started a precipitous decline. The canneries shut down one by one, until the last closed on Cannery Row in 1973. There were several initial ideas about why the sardine fishery collapsed, with the leading reason simply being overfishing. But

Figure 152. The sardine fishery was the largest in the Western Hemisphere from the mid-1920s until about 1950. Photo Sardine King sardine label collection.

because the sardine decline seemed to parallel the increased use of the pesticide DDT in the adjacent Salinas Valley, whose runoff emptied into Monterey Bay, others believed that the accumulation of DDT in the food chain was the culprit.

More recent analysis of longer-term observations now point to the large-scale oceanographic changes throughout the Pacific Ocean as a more likely explanation for the rise and fall of sardine populations. Scientists have found that the collapse in the sardine stocks can be linked to change from warm to colder waters off of the California coast, which in turn were linked to a sharp rise in the number of anchovy, a colder-water fish. As was described in Chapter Three, the entire Pacific Ocean undergoes multi-decadal cycles, which have been designated as the warmer and cooler phases of the Pacific Decadal Oscillation (PDO), where ocean currents and water temperatures, rainfall, fish catches, and sea bird populations all fluctuate. During the warmer phases, El Niño events tend to dominate, water temperatures are warmer, rainfall is greater, and the sardines are plentiful (Figure 153). A warm phase of the PDO dominated from the 1920s to about 1945, which was the heyday of the sardine industry along the California coast. Catches dropped off quickly as we entered a cooler phase of the PDO, and the anchovies returned. A new warm phase of the PDO began in 1978 and, not surprisingly in retrospect, the sardine populations rebounded, although the taste and market for sardines never attained its earlier Cannery Row levels. Scientists have found that sardine catches as far apart as California, Peru, and Japan followed parallel courses, and when they collapsed, anchovy returned in a regular cycle that could not be explained simply by overfishing. So fish populations, as well as sea birds and other components of the oceanic food chain, are tied to regular cycles in ocean circulation that we still are working to understand. The questions that remain include what is driving these basin-wide changes and when might they change next?

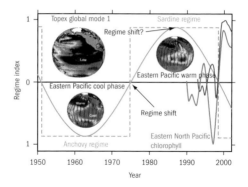

Figure 153. The relative abundance of either sardines or anchovies off California is related to Pacific Decadal Oscillation cycles. Provided by Francisco Chavez, Monteray Bay Aquarium Research Institute.

Looking Offshore: Some Final Thoughts

The continental shelf is the drowned edge of the coast of California and has been alternately exposed and flooded during the constantly alternating glacial and interglacial periods of the past several million years. The last glacial era ended about 18,000 years ago, and as the glaciers retreated and ice shelves melted, sea level rose again and moved the shoreline landward to where it is today. What we see is temporary, however, and all indications are that sea level will continue to rise, moving the shoreline landward for many decades into the future.

The continental shelf and its many submarine canyons lie hidden beneath the ocean today, but have now been imaged with high-tech multi-beam bathymetry, which has allowed us for the first time to see the offshore seafloor in three dimensions. There are both energy and living marine resources offshore, and California has exploited these to a high degree, providing the state with the largest ocean economy in the

United States. There are limits to many of these resources, however, as well as costs and impacts of extraction or utilization, and a combination of human actions and natural cycles has had profound effects on the availability and sustainability of many of these.

Losing Ground: The Effects of a Rising Sea Level

If you've ever watched storm waves batter the coastline in the winter months, you can appreciate the tremendous power exerted by the ocean. Even during calm weather, small waves constantly wash the sand and gravel across the intertidal zone—wetting, drying, and gradually weakening the rocks that make up the base of the sea cliff and carrying off the bits and pieces that break loose. Although this day-to-day activity takes its toll on the cliffs or bluffs, it is generally the winter storm waves at times of high tides that lead to the greatest coastal retreat. In part, this is because the winter waves are larger and have more energy. In addition, prolonged winter rains weaken the bluffs or cliffs, often making them more susceptible to failure. Another important factor is the reduction in width or even the total disappearance of protective beaches during winter. With this buffer zone of sand reduced or gone, the waves can attack the cliffs, bluffs, or dunes more frequently and with greater energy.

During severe winters we often see television news reports or read newspaper stories about houses or roads being undermined or collapsing into the ocean (Figure 154). Shoreline erosion is a logical consequence of continuing sea level rise due to global warming. The consequence of the sea level rise of the past 18,000 years was initially a gradual and progressive flooding of California's continental shelf and includes what we witness today, the continuing landward migration or retreat of the shoreline. Sea level rise is not a big concern in undeveloped coastal areas, but for the populated coastlines of the world, the inland migration of the shoreline has an enormous impact. Today there are about 100 million people living within three feet of sea level, and three feet of sea level rise by 2100 is certainly within our range of reasonable probability. Although this is not of much concern if you

Figure 154. Several houses built on the beach along the shoreline of Monterey Bay collapsed onto the sand during the 1983 winter when beach scour exceeded the depth of the pilings. Photo Gary Griggs.

live in Fresno or Bakersfield, oceanfront property owners as well as local governments have some pressing issues to deal with in the years ahead.

In 2008, the state of California as well as several coastal communities were beginning to develop adaptation and longer-term mitigation plans to deal with a rising sea level. Mitigation includes measures that could be taken by government agencies, businesses, or individuals to reduce local greenhouse gas emissions, thereby reducing their individual community impacts on global warming. Adaptation includes any approaches or actions that will begin to reduce the effects or impacts that global warming will have on an individual community or region. Potential impacts include beach inundation, cliff and bluff erosion leading to increased coastal storm damage and infrastructure and property loss, enhanced seawater intrusion, and changes in precipitation patterns, thereby potentially affecting water availability and flooding. For coastal development and infrastructure, how high might sea level rise by 2025, or

2050? Where might the shoreline be as a result? How about the uncertainty of whether warmer water and changing weather will bring more frequent coastal storms? These are all serious and difficult questions to try to resolve. There is no simple and universal set of adaptation responses as of this writing, but many ideas are being put forward. Adapting to flooding and inundation with a continued rise in sea level is a much different challenge than adapting to continued cliff retreat, for example. Retreating, armoring, and elevating structures are some of the responses to sea level rise and shoreline retreat that have been used along the California coast over the past century, but will these work in the decades ahead?

Worn at the Edges: How Does the Coastline Erode?

Erosion along the coast of California can take several different forms. The beach erodes seasonally, but this is a reversible process, and the beach sand lost each winter is generally replaced by the next summer (Figure 115). As discussed in Chapter Five, where a wide sandy beach has historically fronted the coast, but sand supplies have been significantly reduced through the construction of dams or large coastal engineering structures, then the beach itself can be permanently eroded or narrowed. There is concern that some southern California beaches may be undergoing long-term erosion owing to sand-supply reduction. The beach may be rebuilt and recover, however, if sand supplies or sand flow are restored.

Coastal erosion is the actual landward retreat of the coastal cliff, bluff, or dune. This process is distinct from beach erosion and is not recoverable, at least within our lifetimes or by natural processes. The rate at which any back-beach feature erodes, whether a cliff, bluff, or dune, depends on several different factors, including the rate of regional sea level rise. A second is the amount of wave energy reaching that particular area of coastline, as well as the physical properties of the materials that make up the cliff, bluff, or dune. In a rock cliff, the physical properties include the hardness or degree of consolidation or cementation of the cliff rock. The presence of internal weaknesses such as fractures, joints, or faults also directly affects the resistance of the rock to wave impact, as does the degree of chemical weathering of the rock by seawater.

Cliff erosion takes place through several different processes, all gradually taking their toll on private or public oceanfront property. Hydraulic impact is perhaps the most important and is simply the direct impact of a breaking wave on the cliff (Figure 155). Where rocks are unconsolidated or jointed, waves can dislodge large and small fragments or blocks, leading to gradual failure or retreat of the cliff. The sand, gravel, and even cobbles that the waves wash back and

Figure 155. Most coastal storm damage occurs during times of high tides and large storm waves. Photo Deepika Shrestha Ross.

forth across the shoreline become important abrasion tools. The constant grinding of the rocks against the bedrock works just like sandpaper. Gravel and cobbles can be hurled against the cliffs under large wave conditions, further contributing to cliff breakdown and retreat. The alternating daily and seasonal cycles of wetting and drying, and heating and cooling, that take place within rocks in the intertidal zone, as well as the chemical breakdown of the rocks by seawater, are also important processes. The bedrock exposed in cliffs and along the shoreline is broken down by a combination of physical disaggregation and chemical reaction. All these processes act in concert to either weaken the cliff-forming materials or break out and remove individual fragments.

The impacts of urbanization, such as street or storm drain runoff, septic tank leaching, landscape watering, and the alteration of normal runoff away from natural drainages so that more water passes through or across the cliffs, also contribute to accelerated cliff or bluff retreat. Each process can erode the cliff directly or lead to weakening of the

Figure 156. Cliffs in the Depot Hill area of Capitola continue to fail as the base of the cliff is undermined by wave scour. A road along the top of the cliff has been gradually lost to collapse. Photo Gary Griggs.

cliff material followed by slumping or sliding (Figure 156). Although native vegetation usually acts to stabilize sea cliffs, planting nonnative or ornamental vegetation in some instances has had the opposite effect. Excessive watering may weaken the cliff-top materials. The roots of some trees may penetrate into fractures, joints, or weak zones in the rocks and act as wedges to pry away large blocks. In addition, ground cover, such as ice plant, often hangs down over the cliff with so much weight that it uproots and carries down soil and loose cliff-top material with it.

Coastlines consisting of hard crystalline rock, such as the granite of the Monterey Peninsula, Point Lobos, or the outer end of Point Reyes, usually erode very slowly. Within these resistant materials, however, erosion rates may still vary. Waves attack the weaker zones such as fractures and joints to

Figure 157. The homes at Gleason's Beach along the Sonoma County coast were built on a narrow strip between State Hwy. 1 and an unstable cliff. The coastline is very irregular due to differences in the resistance of the Franciscan bedrock to wave attack. Seawalls actually retain the septic tanks on the beach at the base of the bluff. Photo Kenneth and Gabrielle Adelman, California Coastal Records Project, www.CaliforniaCoastline.org.

form inlets and coves. Good examples of the influence of rock resistance variability on wave attack occur along the coasts of Sonoma (Figure 157), Mendocino, and Humboldt counties, as well as the Big Sur coast. The geological variability typified by the Franciscan Formation, which is a chaotic mixture of very hard rocks (such as cherts, which resist wave attack), and softer mudstones and shales (which are more easily eroded) produces a very irregular coastline. The more resistant rock remains in the form of points, headlands, or offshore sea stacks, whereas the weaker rocks erode to form embayments (Figure 157). In contrast, erosion can be uniformly rapid where the coastline is made up of relatively soft, weak sedimentary rock such as sandstone or shale, or even unconsolidated materials. In these zones, the cliffs often retreat in a more linear fashion, producing relatively straight coasts such as the shoreline from Santa Barbara to Point Conception and from Santa Cruz to Half Moon Bay (Figure 158).

Coastal cliff retreat is one of the more dramatic processes taking place along the coastline. Undermined foundations,

Figure 158. The coastline along this portion of San Mateo County is very linear due to the uniform nature of the sedimentary rocks that make up the cliff. The accumulation of talus at the base of the cliff and the lack of vegetation indicate that this cliff is actively eroding. Photo Gary Griggs.

Figure 159. Continued retreat of the sea cliff in Isla Vista near the University of California Santa Barbara campus has progressively undermined the foundations of these apartments. Photo Gary Griggs.

dangling decks and stairways, and structures that have collapsed onto the beach are harsh reminders of the ongoing retreat of the California coastline (Figure 159). Many coastal communities have lost entire oceanfront streets through continuing erosion over the years. There are also many former lots that now lie beneath the waves.

The retreat or erosion of California's coastal bluffs and cliffs is due not only to waves gnawing at the cliff base, but also to landsliding, slumping, and rockfalls originating higher on the cliff. For example, the combination of jointing patterns in the bedrock, wedging by tree roots, and undercutting by waves has led to regular rockfalls from the sea cliffs along what is locally known as Depot Hill between the city of Capitola and New Brighton State Beach along the shoreline of northern Monterey Bay (Figure 160). These failures commonly occur after intense storms, when rainfall and runoff have been high and the surf heavy. In March 1983, a slab 100 feet long and six to 12 feet wide collapsed and fell to

Figure 160. Failure of the sandstone and mudstone along these northern Monterey Bay cliffs occurs as large, joint-bounded blocks fail, and has produced an average annual erosion rate of about one foot per year. Runoff from the developed cliff top area has probably contributed to the failure. Photo Gary Griggs.

the beach below, removing part of a city street. Cliff failure a decade earlier at this same location led to the relocation of a two-story house to a safer site two blocks inland. During the 1989 magnitude 7.0 Loma Prieta earthquake, additional cliff failure occurred and six cliff-top apartments had to be demolished in the same area. Seismic shaking during this major earthquake triggered rockfalls and bluff failures from Marin County to Monterey Bay, a distance of over 100 miles. At long-term average erosion rates of about a foot per year, an oceanfront street that formerly existed along this stretch of cliff top has now almost completely disappeared.

Landslides or slope failures can be much larger than the Capitola example, as illustrated by the Portuguese Bend landslide in the Palos Verdes Hills along the Los Angeles coastline. In this massive failure, which covered about half a square mile, movement began in 1956 and continued for a number of years (Figure 27). More than 200 homes were destroyed or damaged in this event, and property damage amounted to about $78 million (in 2008 dollars).

Large coastal landslides are frequent along the Big Sur coast because of weaknesses of the rocks exposed, the very steep slopes, and high rainfall. Many slides extend from the ridge tops to the shoreline and also involve California Hwy. 1, which is a challenge to keep open during years of heavy rainfall. Prolonged rainfall tends to initiate or reactivate these slides. They present problems for any type of land use because landslides of this scale are very difficult and expensive to stabilize or eliminate. Removal and repair costs to the state of California for one large Big Sur landslide in the mid-1980s were over $13 million (in 2008 dollars) and required the removal of three million cubic yards of material (Figure 23). There have been dozens of these along this stretch of coastline. They occur so often in the same places that Cal Trans has given them all names: Grandpa's Elbow, McWay, J.P. Burns, and Cow Cliffs, as well as many others.

Devil's Slide, about six miles north of Half Moon Bay and five miles south of Pacifica, is another example of the challenges of maintaining a major state highway across an active coastal landslide (Figure 161). Construction of the road began in 1935 and took two years to complete. The first major landslide destroyed much of the road in 1940, and an ongoing cycle of destruction and rebuilding has gone on ever since. One of the longest closures took place in 1995, lasted 158 days, and cost over $4 million (in 2008 dollars) to repair. After decades of closures and repairs, and also debates about solutions, two bypass tunnels, each 30 feet wide and 4,200 feet long are now being constructed beneath San Pedro Mountain and are projected for completion in 2010 (Figure 162).

The Big Rock Mesa slide along the Malibu coast is a steep hillside area developed with homes that has closed the Pacific Coast Highway on more than one occasion (Figure 163). In

Figure 161. State Hwy. 1 has always had a precarious existence in the Devil's Slide area of San Mateo County with frequent landslides and hillside failure. Photo Kenneth and Gabrielle Adelman, California Coastal Records Project, www.CaliforniaCoastline.org.

Figure 162. A long tunnel though the coastal mountains is now under construction that will allow Hwy. 1 to bypass Devil's Slide. Photo Kenneth and Gabrielle Adelman, California Coastal Records Project, www.CaliforniaCoastline.org.

Figure 163. The Big Rock Slide along the steep slopes of the Santa Monica Mountains in the Malibu area threatened homes and the highway until it was stabilized. Photo Kenneth and Gabrielle Adelman, California Coastal Records Project, www.CaliforniaCoastline.org.

this case, it appears to have been an ancient landslide that was reactivated by groundwater seepage from heavy rains in 1979 that first closed the highway and destroyed some homes. In the El Niño winter of 1983 about 200 acres were displaced, leading to condemnation of 13 homes and threats to hundreds of others. This triggered extensive geological investigations, expensive stabilization measures, and extended lawsuits.

On January 10, 2005, a massive landslide and earth flow struck the community of La Conchita, midway between Ventura and Santa Barbara, destroying or seriously damaging 36 houses and killing 10 people (Figure 164). Sadly, a large landslide had inundated the community just 10 years earlier and had destroyed or seriously damaged nine houses. The small community of about 200 homes lies on a narrow coastal strip between the Pacific Coast Highway and a steep, 600-foot-high bluff. The sedimentary rocks exposed in the bluff are weakly cemented and the entire area has a history of landsliding

Figure 164. The high, steep cliffs behind La Conchita, north of Ventura, have failed twice in recent years, destroying homes and taking lives. Photo Bruce Perry, CSULB Geological Sciences.

dating back at least to 1865. The Southern Pacific Railroad passes along the coastal bench and was inundated by debris from landsliding in 1889 and again in 1909, when an entire train was buried. The 2005 slide and mudflow was triggered by two weeks of record rainfall in southern California with the closest city to the south, Ventura, getting nearly 15 inches of rain in that two week period. Mud from the failure flowed down the streets of La Conchita and crossed the Pacific Coast Highway, trapping vehicles for hours.

A Rapid Retreat: How Fast Is the Coastline Eroding?

The shape of the California coast we see today at any particular location reflects the ability of the materials making up the bluff or cliff to resist the forces that are acting to break down the coast. Other things being equal, the rocks which are the hardest and, therefore, most resistant to erosion, granite, for example, stand out as points or promontories.

The interaction of the physical processes that produce cliff erosion or retreat (earthquakes, wave exposure, rainfall, and runoff) with all the varied types of rocks exposed along the shoreline have resulted in wide-ranging erosion rates along California's 1,100 miles of coastline. At some sites, the granite of Point Lobos or the Monterey peninsula, for example, cliff erosion has been negligible for the past 75 to 100 years, simply because the rocks are so hard and resist wave attack. Elsewhere the average rate of retreat may be as high as five to 10 feet per year. At Point Año Nuevo, in southern San Mateo County, the erosion rate of the low bluffs has averaged about nine feet per year for the last 300 years, one of the highest rates along the state's entire coastline. The low bluffs at this point are only several feet above sea level, so that storm waves can easily reach and erode the material. In general, weaker sedimentary rocks such as sandstones, siltstones, mudstones, and shales that form much of California's coastline retreat at long-term average rates of a few inches to perhaps a foot or more per year in some places (Figure 165). The sand dunes of southern Monterey Bay is another location where the unconsolidated sand of these older dunes offers almost no resistance to wave attack. While historically protected by a wide sandy beach, years of sand mining from the beach has disturbed the long-term balance and increased the frequency with which waves attack the base of the dunes leading to erosion rates as high as five to six feet each year (Figure 166).

Coastal erosion also tends to be episodic, with much of the long-term failure or retreat taking place during a few severe storm events every five or 10 years. The arrival of large storm waves at times of high tides and elevated sea

Figure 165. These poorly consolidated sandy bluffs at Pacifica offer little protection for the bluff top apartments and little resistance to wave attack. Photo Gary Griggs

Figure 166. These unconsolidated sand dunes at the former Fort Ord along the shoreline of Southern Monterey Bay erode at rates of five to six feet per year. Rock and rubble was dumped regularly at the base of the bluff in order to protect Stillwell Hall but erosion continued to either side. The building was demolished when the base was closed. Photo Kenneth and Gabrielle Adelman, California Coastal Records Project, www.CaliforniaCoastline.org.

levels, which frequently occur during major El Niño events, can produce severe coastal erosion in areas formerly thought to be relatively stable. For example, erosion in the resistant sandstones and siltstones at Sunset Cliffs, San Diego, had averaged about a half an inch per year for the 75-year period prior to 1973, and most of this area had undergone no significant erosion during this period. In 1976, however, the U.S. Army Corps of Engineers reported that at the foot of Del Mar Street, Sunset Cliffs, the top of the bluff had retreated landward 40 feet between 1962 and 1976, averaging about 2.7 feet per year. Although the average retreat of the cliffs above Capitola in northern Monterey Bay is about one foot per year, large slabs may collapse overnight, suddenly moving the cliff edge back five to 10 feet, followed by little change for a number of years (Figure 156). Short-term cliff erosion rates may often be much different from long-term (30 to 50-year) averages.

Living on the Edge: The Hazards of Oceanfront Living

Anyone who has ever stood on the edge of a low coastal bluff during a winter storm does not need to be convinced that the coastline is a dynamic environment (Figure 167). Unfortunately, however, most coastal properties and homes are bought and sold during the warm, calm days of summer, when there are no obvious threats to these parcels. Coastal change occurs both over short time intervals (the impact from a single storm or winter, for example) and over longer intervals (the progressive erosion of an unstable bluff area over years or decades).

Even though it has been discussed in earlier chapters, it is important to stress again here that the coast or shoreline of California is a temporary line in the sand. We have built homes and apartments, streets and sewer lines, hotels

Figure 167. Large waves breaking up and over the sea cliff during the winter present a different hazard than during the calm days of summer. Photo Deepika Shrestha Ross.

and restaurants, parks and parking lots, and entire communities right at the water's edge within a few feet of sea level (Figure 168). Yet sea level is constantly changing, primarily in response to climate change. The 350- to 400-foot rise in sea level that resulted from the melting of ice caps and glaciers at the end of the last Ice Age is still underway.

Figure 168. Newport Beach, like portions of many southern California beach communities, was built directly on the sand. Photo Kenneth and Gabrielle Adelman, California Coastal Records Project, www. CaliforniaCoastline.org.

Now superimposed on top of the natural climatic cycles is the impact of human activity, primarily the production of greenhouse gases, which has accelerated the global warming process, further raising sea level. Because greenhouse gases in the atmosphere will remain for several hundred years, the effects of our past emissions will be with us for centuries.

Unfortunately, however, the increasing industrialization of global society is releasing more of these gases, and their concentration is going to increase for decades before we begin to agree internationally how we are going to substantially reduce these emissions.

California's coastline, like nearly every other coastline around the world, is retreating in response to a rising sea level and will continue to retreat for many decades to come. As discussed earlier in this chapter, the coastal landforms and underlying geological materials, combined with the relative sea level rise and wave climate at any individual location, determines how fast any particular section of California's coastline will retreat. The impacts of the ongoing coastline erosion are directly related to the type and intensity of development. Along California's wild and mostly undeveloped sections of coastline, primarily Del Norte, Humboldt, Sonoma, and Mendocino counties in the north, and parts of San Mateo, Santa Cruz, Monterey, and San Luis Obispo counties along the central coast, the coastline can migrate inland for some distance before there are any large losses. State Hwy. 1 is an exception, and much of this scenic highway's route lies perilously close to the edge (Figure 161). In 2008 CalTrans developed a plan to relocate Hwy. 1 inland near San Simeon, and a tunnel is being built to relocate the highway away from the eroding cliffs at the Devil's Slide area north of Half Moon Bay (Figure 162).

Along California's developed coastline there are three physical or geomorphic environments where widespread development has taken place and where past and future retreat will continue to be a serious concern: (1) the beach itself, (2) sand dunes, and (3) eroding cliffs or bluffs.

Building on the Sand: Beach Construction

Houses and many other structures have been built directly on the beach along the California shoreline. Some homes are on concrete slabs directly on the beach, and others are elevated on pilings above the sand and surrounding driftwood (Figure 169). These sandy back-beach areas are similar to the flat floodplains adjacent to creeks and rivers. Just as floods overflow stream banks and inundate the floodplains during major rainstorms, large waves combined with high tides periodically sweep completely across the beach and up to the flanking sea cliff or dunes. This inundation may

Figure 169. Many houses along the Malibu coast were built out over the beach on caissons or pilings. Photo Kenneth and Gabrielle Adelman, California Coastal Records Project, www.CaliforniaCoastline.org.

not happen every winter, but it is important to realize how the sand, driftwood, and other storm debris was left in front of and under those beach front homes or other structures. It may not have occurred last winter, but the evidence is a reminder that it has happened before and will happen again, and probably more frequently in the future.

Stinson Beach in Marin County, Pot Belly Beach, Las Olas Drive, and Beach Drive in Santa Cruz County, Oxnard Shores in Ventura County, Broad Beach in Malibu, the beach front communities of Los Angeles County such as Santa Monica, Venice, Playa Del Rey, Manhattan, and Hermosa Beach, as well as Newport Beach, Del Mar, Mission Beach, and Imperial Beach, are all communities or areas that have oceanfront development on the beach or within a few feet of high tide (Figure 170). Along the Malibu shoreline there is even a street named Sea Level Drive (Figure 63), and in Monterey we have streets named Spray and Wave Crest! Construction at these addresses may bring some future surprises not anticipated when the streets were originally named.

Figure 170. Homes in the Mission Beach area of San Diego were built essentially at beach level. Photo Kenneth and Gabrielle Adelman, California Coastal Records Project, www.CaliforniaCoastline.org.

The state's entire coastline experienced higher than predicted tides, frequent storm surges, and large waves that produced oceanfront damage from one end of the state to the other in the major ENSO or El Niño years of 1978, 1983, and 1997–98. In 1983, 12 to 15 major storms with very large waves (over 10 feet in height) reached the California coast during January, February, and March. Seven storms coincided with very high tides. As a result, much of the beach sand was removed by waves during the first day or two of these storms. With this natural buffer or shock absorber gone, the wave energy from subsequent storms eroded the beaches further and then attacked the low-lying areas along the shoreline with greater force, increasing the impacts on back-beach structures and property. As a result, the 1983 damage was perhaps the most severe in half a century. Damage included undermining of shallow pilings or piers so that homes on the beach collapsed onto the sand. Structures on low pilings were also uplifted by waves at high tide and smashed through the pilings as they fell. In addition, waves overtopped low,

Figure 171. A row of homes was built on fill above the beach in the Aptos area of northern Monterey Bay. During the elevated sea levels, high tides, and storm waves of the 1983 El Niño, waves washed up the revetment and damaged and destroyed the fronts of many of the homes. Photo Gary Griggs.

protective seawalls or other barriers and either flooded, damaged, or destroyed the home fronts or other structures facing the sea (Figure 171). In some cases structural damage of this sort led to house collapse. Nonstructural damage, such as the loss of decks, stairways, patios, yards, and landscaping, was widespread.

An unexpected southeaster brought strong winds and extremely large waves to southern California beaches on January 17 and 18, 1988. The measured wave heights from this exceptional storm exceeded anything ever recorded along the southern California coast. The Redondo Beach–King Harbor area was severely damaged by large waves that found a route through the normally sheltering offshore Channel Islands. Wave energy within the harbor was severe enough to destroy the front of the Portofino Hotel, and 54 guests had to be evacuated by helicopters as waves washed a barge into the bottom floor. The yacht club, two restaurants, and many shops located on Horseshoe Pier also suffered heavy damage. Low-lying construction at Mission Beach near San Diego was also inundated as beaches from Santa Barbara to San Diego lost 75 to 150 feet of beach width during the two-day storm.

Beach construction along much of the Malibu coast took place during the calmer and cooler phase of the Pacific Decadal Oscillation, which lasted from about 1945 until 1977. In places like Broad Beach, houses were built directly on the sand of this wide beach. With the weather changes accompanying the switch to a warmer PDO phase, which began in 1978 and appears to have continued into the present, storm surges, higher sea levels, and more severe waves have damaged and threatened more and more homes that were previously considered high and dry. Now that much of this former broad beach has been removed, residents are now faced with the uncertainties of what lies ahead, and how and how long they can protect their beach-level homes (Figure 172).

Figure 172. The shoreline at Broad Beach in Malibu has retreated in recent years, and sand bags and plastic have been used as for temporary protection. Photo Deepika Shrestha Ross.

As sea level continues to rise in the years and decades ahead, inundation and storm damage to construction and development on the back-beach will become more frequent. Adapting to sea level rise will have to be given much more serious consideration than it has in the past and will be a challenge to all of California's communities with beach-level construction for years to come.

Blown Away: Building on the Dunes

Because California's coast is geologically young and tectonically active, much of it is characterized by coastal mountains, steep cliffs, and low bluffs, occasionally broken by stream valleys or low coastal plains. As a result, sand dunes, which need a relatively flat, low-lying area to form on, are somewhat restricted along California's coast. The older and geologically more stable, low-relief south Atlantic and Gulf coasts of the United States, by contrast, have far more extensive sand dune development.

The primary dunes, or those closest to the ocean and tied to the beach for their sand supply, must be understood as works in progress. These dunes are always on the move. Although there may be older dunes farther inland that have been stabilized by vegetation and no longer depend on the beach for fresh sand, the oceanfront dunes change regularly. Storm waves cut away at the base of the dunes during the winter months, and summer wind and swell bring the sand back onto the beach to help rebuild the dunes. During severe winters the most seaward dunes may be severely eroded or breached altogether.

Dune stability is easily affected by human intervention, as exemplified along stretches of the New Jersey coast. Houses were built on conventional foundations atop beachfront dunes, destroying the grasses and other stabilizing vegetation. These dunes were breached to provide vehicle and human access to the beach, groundwater was withdrawn for landscape watering, and large areas were paved over for streets and parking. In March 1962, a violent nor'easter attacked the entire Atlantic Coast with 60-mile-per-hour winds combined with high tides and large waves. In a matter of a few days, 2,400 homes were destroyed or damaged beyond repair. Foundation exposure was the most common problem. Those houses that sat high on the dunes, with the best views, found the sand swept out from under them until their foundations or pilings collapsed or were damaged beyond repair.

There are some extensive dune fields along California's coast (see Chapter Two), although those that have been developed are usually difficult to recognize as dunes by the casual observer. The extensive dune fields of the San Francisco peninsula and the El Segundo were progressively urbanized over the years such that little of these once migrating sand fields are still visible (Figure 173). San Francisco's Ocean Beach provided the sand that blew dunes inland all the way to the bay. In 1868 the city of San Francisco set aside the land for Golden Gate Park along with a strip of land along the shoreline for use by the public. Some improvements were made as the area became more popular, which included sand fences in attempts to keep the sand from blowing inland. In response to increasing public use, the Great Highway was improved in 1915 by paving over the dune closest to the beach. When the massive O'Shaughnessy seawall was constructed in 1929, the present Great Highway was completed, along with parking areas and access to the ocean. The seawall more or less permanently stabilized the shoreline, but also cut off the sand supply to the dunes, and because the highway was elevated, prevented sand from blowing up onto the roadway (Figure 174).

One of the most extensive areas of home development on oceanfront dunes in California can be found in central Monterey Bay just north of Moss Landing. Although the

Figure 173. The Los Angeles International Airport is underlain by sand dunes, some of which are still visible at the end of the runway. Photo Kenneth and Gabrielle Adelman, California Coastal Records Project, www.CaliforniaCoastline.org.

Figure 174. When the Great Highway and O'Shaughnessy Seawall were built along Ocean Beach in San Francisco in 1929, the source of sand for the inland dunes was cut off. Photo Kenneth and Gabrielle Adelman, California Coastal Records Project, www.CaliforniaCoastline.org.

developed dune area is relatively small (a total of about two miles of oceanfront) compared with East Coast dune development, the problems and hazards are identical. Where individual homes, townhouses, and condominiums were built on conventional foundations and directly on the frontal or primary dune, periodic wave erosion has threatened and partially undermined the buildings. Since construction began at the Pajaro Dunes development in 1969, severe storms have threatened major portions of this frontal dune development during three different winters, all El Niño years. Up to 40 feet of dune erosion occurred during the winter of 1983 at this location. Structures were threatened, foundations were undermined, and over $4 million (in 2008 dollars) worth of emergency rock was brought in and quickly piled against the eroding dune face to protect the structures (Figure 38).

A large, 172-unit apartment complex was built on the dunes just about a mile and a half north of the city of Monterey between 1972 and 1974, where long-term dune erosion rates were one to two feet per year. The oceanfront units were initially threatened by the large waves, high tides, and elevated sea levels of the 1982–83 El Niño. Wave erosion broke the water line, which had to be rerouted, and threatened the sewer and electrical lines. Continuing dune erosion by January 1984 had come to within 14 feet of the shallow wooden pilings supporting the apartments. Five thousand tons of rocks were brought in to provide emergency protection, but because the apartments were built right to the property line, the rock had to be placed on city beach (Figure 175). Ultimately, the city required that the emergency rock be removed in order to allow beach goers to walk along the beach. Continued dune retreat and concern with structural support led to a major engineering effort to support the frontal units, with a series of 50-foot deep concrete piers connected by grade beams (Figure 176). Although the shoreline has advanced and

Figure 175. The Ocean Harbor House apartments in the city of Monterey were built on the dunes very close to the shoreline. Severe erosion during the 1983 El Niño winter cut back the dunes and threatened the shallow pilings that supported the buildings. Emergency riprap was brought in for temporary protection in 1984. Photo Gary Griggs.

Figure 176. Following removal of the emergency riprap and continued erosion, the outer units of Ocean Harbor House were supported with concrete piers and grade beams. As erosion continued, emergency riprap was again installed in 2004, 20 years after the first emergency riprap. Photo Gary Griggs.

retreated seasonally, the overall pattern has been one of continuing retreat of the dune edge at an average rate of nearly two feet per year.

The 1997–98 El Niño caused additional retreat, and by 2002 more emergency rock had to be emplaced to prevent undermining of additional units. As part of a 2004 Environmental Impact Report process, property owners and their consultants considered many different proposals for protecting the threatened structures and evaluated the environmental impacts of each. The proposal that the owners favored was a shotcrete seawall, textured to look like an eroded sand dune. It was recognized by the California Coastal Commission that sea level rise and continued shoreline retreat would ultimately lead to complete loss of the beach as well as alongshore access. As a mitigation measure the property owners were required to provide the funds to nourish the beach in front of the structure or provide suitable replacement. While the seawall was under construction in 2008, the mitigation fee issue has worked its way to the United States Supreme Court. The conflict between the protection of private oceanfront property and the impacts of those protection measures on the public beach has been an ongoing issue in California for several decades.

Stinson Beach and Seadrift in Marin County are also areas where homes have been built over the years on the low sand dunes immediately landward of the beach. During the 1983 El Niño winter, high tides, elevated sea levels, and repeated storms damaged some of these low-lying structures. The dunes fronting the beach anywhere along the California coast should be seen as active, moving landforms with no guarantee of long-term stability. With a continuing rise in sea level and the accompanying shoreline migration, the dunes will also move landward where the topography allows, leaving any structures or infrastructure behind (Figure 177).

A

B

Figure 177. Photographs looking south at Ocean Harbor House in 1984 (A) and 2004 (B) showing progressive erosion of the dunes and exposure of additional pipe and concrete. Photo Gary Griggs.

Eroding Cliffs and Bluffs: The Cost of a 180-Degree Ocean View

Uplifted marine terraces dominate along well over half of California's coastline. These nearly flat benches, commonly up to a mile or more in width, have proven to be convenient sites for development. The coastal bluffs and cliffs that form the outer edges of these terraces have been intensively developed with single-family homes, condominiums, apartments, hotels, motels, and restaurants throughout much of southern California. The terraced coastline from Del Mar to Leucadia, as well as Solana Beach, Newport Beach, Palos Verdes, and parts of the Santa Barbara and Goleta coast (Figure 31), have been moderately to intensively developed. Although the urbanization of the ocean-front bluffs and cliffs is far less intense along the state's central and north coast because population densities are lower, these oceanfront cliffs have been developed locally in communities such as Pismo Beach, Morro Bay, Cayucos, San Simeon, Rio del Mar, Capitola, Santa Cruz, and Half Moon Bay. Farther north, the picturesque Victorian town of Mendocino (Figure 26) and the lumber towns of Fort Bragg and Crescent City have all been built on the lowest marine terrace.

All these developed bluffs and cliffs are at the mercy of winter wave attack. The bluff edges are all migrating landward, but at different rates depending on the interaction of the waves, tides, rainfall, and earthquakes with the rocks or materials that make up the cliffs. Coastal geologists have documented bluff retreat rates as high as five to six feet per year, but we also have evidence of much more resistant areas where there has been no detectable change in the past 50 to 75 years. Where average cliff retreat rates are a foot or more annually, serious problems face any home or property owner. On the other hand, where retreat rates are very low, homes or parcels may be secure for decades to come, depending in large part on future sea level rise rates and storm or wave climate in the years ahead. Large earthquakes, although relatively infrequent and unpredictable, can also initiate large-scale cliff failure (Figure 6).

Coastal cliffs may slump or fail as small masses or fragments, as large, often joint-bounded bocks, or as massive slides or slumps. Evidence of recent cliff failure is often easily recognized as fresh or non-vegetated scars on the cliffs themselves, or as blocks or debris at the base of the cliff (Figure 156). This type of evidence should alert present or prospective property owners to potential erosion and failure problems.

Other general observations or evidence can be useful as well. For example, cliffs that consist of layered sedimentary rock, such as shale, and where the bedding or layering is tilted down toward the beach, are notoriously unstable, and large slabs will frequently break loose and slide or fall to the beach below. Undermined, subsiding, or cracked roads, sidewalks, or patios near the cliff edge likely reflect recent or progressive failure of the underlying materials. The age or maturity of the vegetation on the cliffs may also provide evidence of stability or recent history. Although there are many rocky cliffs that do not support vegetation, unvegetated cliffs or bluffs or those with only very young or immature vegetation may have suffered recent failure or erosion. In contrast, older trees often suggest at least some extended period of stability.

There are many stories of horror and disaster along these developed but eroding cliffs and bluffs that form over half of the state's coastline. Gleason's Beach along the Sonoma coast is a row of what were originally 20 homes constructed about 40 or 50 years ago on a narrow strip of eroding cliff on the ocean side of State Hwy. 1. The underlying

Franciscan bedrock is a mixture of very resistant rocks that form points and offshore sea stacks, and much weaker mudstones and shales, which are highly prone to landsliding. Several homes have been destroyed or have suffered serious foundation problems as the unstable slopes have failed, and other homes have been undermined. Seawalls and retaining walls have been built in an attempt to save the remaining structures (Figure 178).

Forty miles south and lying almost astride the San Andreas Fault, the small community of Bolinas was originally settled in the 1880s, and the erosion of the steep cliffs has been a never-ending hazard ever since. The bedrock is weak and septic tank leaching as well as the infiltration of winter rain reduces the strength of the underlying shales, which leads to slope failures. Although many homes line the bluff edge, it

Figure 178. Several houses have been destroyed or removed as erosion has continued at Gleason's Beach along the Sonoma County coast, leaving portions of their foundations behind at the base of the cliff. Photo Kenneth and Gabrielle Adelman, California Coastal Records Project, www.CaliforniaCoastline.org.

has been retreating at about a foot or two per year for over a century. Retaining walls, seawalls, and groins to stabilize the cliff and fronting beach have come and gone, and a handful of houses have been damaged, condemned, and demolished over the years.

South of San Francisco the bluffs in the Daly City and Pacifica areas are covered with a mixture of tract homes as well as apartments, condominiums, and mobile home parks. Weak sands underlie most of these high bluffs (Figure 165), although they are partially protected from wave attack by seasonal beaches. The picture changes in the winter months, however, particularly during those with strong El Niños. Elevated sea levels and large storm waves remove the protective beach and take a toll on the bluff itself. The high bluffs at Daly City suffered major landsliding during the 1989 Loma Prieta earthquake (Figure 6), which was some 75 miles away. It does not take too much imagination to consider what might happen when the section of the San Andreas Fault that passes directly beneath this area ruptures again.

An entire row of homes along the Esplanade in Pacifica was threatened by bluff erosion during the 1983 El Niño. Protective riprap was subsequently placed at the base of the bluff, but when the 1997–98 El Niño hit, the rock had settled into the sand and the waves again battered the weak and now unprotected bluffs. This time an entire row of homes along the bluff edge were undermined (Figure 179) and ultimately demolished (Figure 180).

Farther south, the cliffs forming the coastline of northern Monterey Bay from the Santa Cruz Harbor to Rio Del Mar have been almost completely developed with single-family homes and a few scattered apartments. Pleasure Point, Opal Cliffs, and Depot Hill in Capitola are all areas where homes and infrastructure are threatened by cliff retreat (Figure 181). While the original homes built a century or more ago were typically built with a healthy setback from

Figure 179. These houses on the bluff along the Esplanade in Pacifica, south of San Francisco, were undermined by wave erosion and cliff failure during the 1997 to 1998 El Niño winter. The houses either collapsed onto the beach or were demolished by spring 1998. Photo Monty Hampton, United States Geological Survey.

Figure 180. The Esplanade in Pacifica in 2002 with only two homes remaining. Riprap has been placed at the base of the cliff in an effort to slow additional erosion. Photo Kenneth and Gabrielle Adelman, California Coastal Records Project, www.CaliforniaCoastline.org.

Figure 181. Erosion continues to encroach on these homes in the Opal Cliffs area between the Santa Cruz and Capitola. There is no beach so that waves reach the base of the cliff at most high tides. Photo Kenneth and Gabrielle Adelman, California Coastal Records Project, www.CaliforniaCoastline.org.

the bluff edge, caution was abandoned in the latter half of the twentieth century, and homes were built closer to the edge as ocean views became increasingly more valuable. Riprap and seawalls of one design or another now protect many of these homes. There are others where no protection has been permitted, in part because the Coastal Commission does not yet deem the threats to these homes critical enough. There are no simple solutions, and the storm and wave climate of the next several decades, as well as the rate of sea level rise, are all going to influence the erosion rates and stability of these areas.

Most of the Santa Barbara coastline consists of coastal bluffs eroded into a retreating marine terrace. Isla Vista, the student bedroom community for the adjacent University of California at Santa Barbara campus is perhaps the best example of poorly planned cliff top development with no setbacks or setbacks that have been seriously reduced over time (Figure 31). Student apartments occupy most of the

30-foot-high sea cliff, which consists of weak sedimentary rock. Although a few low-budget cliff protection structures have been built, erosion continues, as the beaches are generally so narrow that waves reach the base of the cliffs at many high tides. The overhanging sections of some apartments have been posted as unsafe to occupy and have been demolished, but new apartments continue to be built on the edge (Figure 159).

Population densities increase moving south along the California coast. The northern San Diego coastline is characterized by marine terraces 25 to 75 feet in height extending from Carlsbad to Del Mar, and it is almost entirely developed. Beaches were generally wider along this stretch of shoreline from the mid-1940s to the mid-1970s, a cooler phase of the Pacific Decadal Oscillation and, therefore, a period with benign weather and little bluff erosion. Permits were issued and homes were built along much of the bluff top during this interval. The climate shifted about 1978 as we entered a warmer phase of the PDO with more intense El Niño events. Beaches narrowed and wave attack, combined with increased groundwater seepage from landscape irrigation, led to undercutting and failure of the lower bluff followed by collapse of the overlying material. The result has been widespread construction of a variety of seawalls, which have provided protection over the short term for many structures.

A large beach nourishment project was carried out in 2001, which added approximately two million cubic yards of offshore sand to 12 beaches along the San Diego coastline at a total cost of $17.5 million (Figure 132). Nearly all this sand tended to move offshore and alongshore with the arrival of winter waves, which should not have come as a surprise. Without regular or repeated nourishment, or the construction of retention structures, such as groins, to stabilize or hold the beach fill, there is no reason why sand added artificially should remain on beaches that were naturally narrow. The considerations that need to be weighed prior to any beach nourishment project are whether the benefits of shoreline sand increases and the potentially short-term or temporary beach-width increases resulting from nourishment are worth the initial investment and continuing costs.

Curious Features on Beaches

Nature has a way of getting our attention, particularly along the shoreline, where there are an endless series of forms and features that can not only be visually striking, but also exhibit a bit of the mysterious or unknown. These might be extremely regular patterns that are repeated along the shoreline, like beach cusps, or odd shaped features or markings on the beach or in the rocks that cause us to stop and wonder. Some of these patterns are widespread, like rills or ripple marks, and can be found on almost any beach, while others, like trace fossils, are hidden in a few special locations. This chapter is a bit different than the others, and is an attempt to try and capture images of some of these shoreline curiosities, and offer at least a partial explanation of why they form in the first place. Many people are happy to just observe these oddities, or to photograph them, but others want to know what went on here. How could such a feature form or originate?

Beach Cusps: Scallops on the Shoreline

Coastal geologists and careful beach observers or frequent visitors may notice evenly spaced, semicircular, scalloped-shaped patterns along the beach face. These very uniform patterns seem to be far more frequent on certain beaches than others and are much more visible from an elevated vantage point, like a cliff top or in an aerial photograph, than when standing on the beach (Figure 182). They can form on sand or gravel beaches and can range in width or diameter from 25 to over 2,000 feet, but are very uniform at any particular location at any point in time (Figure 183). The cusp spacing is shorter in gravel beaches and longer on sandy beaches.

There are many strikingly regular patterns in nature that have long intrigued scientists and non-scientists alike. Beach

Figure 182. Aerial photograph of regularly spaced beach cusps along the northern Monterey Bay shoreline near Seacliff State Beach.

Figure 183. Beach cusps on the shoreline at Seabright Beach in Santa Cruz. Photo Kenneth and Gabrielle Adelman, California Coastal Records Project, www.CaliforniaCoastline.org.

cusps are one of these. They are far easier to recognize and appreciate, however, than to figure out or understand. Published writing on the origin of these features goes back at least 60 years and two different ideas or hypotheses have been put forward for why these unique features form. Neither is easy to explain and both probably will leave some lingering doubts in the minds of most people.

Beach cusps seem to form most often when waves approach normal or at a right angle to the shoreline. The portion of the broken wave that washes up the beach face is called the swash and the maximum difference in the run-up of the swash seems to be the dominant influence on the spacing of the cusps. The earliest idea on the formation of cusps was that they were due to the some distinct properties of the waves breaking on the shoreline and were, therefore, essentially imposed on the beach by nearshore wave interactions.

The alternate concept, which seems to have gained more support recently, is that cusps are the result of a self-organizing process, which serves to create some order along the beach. If we start with a uniform beach face, and there is some irregularity that causes the swash to slow down, perhaps it is a pebble or a piece of driftwood, then the swash will drop some of the coarser or heavier grains it is carrying as it slows. This slightly higher area of roughness will then also decrease the velocity of the next uprush of water, which also drops some of its coarsest sand. This depositional process gradually builds a ridge on the beach surface, which will slow and deflect the swash from each subsequent wave. The ridge or protrusion that builds out is called a horn, and it deflects the swash to either side, which begins to create the bays or scallops. Each of these bays will also cause slight velocity differences as the backwash meets the incoming swash. This helps create the next cusp to either side of the first two embayments. This process then continues to gradually propagate down the beach.

There is an analogy here that may be more readily understandable, which is how a regular washboard pattern forms on an unpaved gravel road. As a car or truck goes over a bump it comes down hard and depresses or compacts the gravel, forming a small depression or trough. Because of the impact, the combination of the weight of the vehicle and the shock absorbers cause the car or truck to come down hard several more times, forming several smaller depressions. When the next vehicle comes along it will bounce over the bump, deepen the depressions and form a few more. After a number of vehicles have gone by, a series of regularly spaced bumps and depressions will have formed, each progressively extending the pattern to gradually create a washboard effect. This seems to be a likely process by which the beach cusps gradually propagate for hundreds or thousands of feet down a beach. Cusps may persist for a few days and, then, due to a change in wave conditions, whether in the size of the waves, or perhaps the direction the waves approach, they will be eroded away by a new swash pattern.

Swash Marks: Covering Your Footprints

As each progressive wave washes up the face of a sandy beach, it is usually carrying some coarser sand, some shells or fragments of shells, as well as small bits of flotsam and jetsam. When the swash reaches its highest point on the beach, some water percolates into the sand, and the rest flows back down the beach face as backwash. At its highest point, the water velocity will drop to zero as the swash reverses flow and begins to move back down towards the water's edge. At this point, where the water is momentarily still, anything being carried by the swash can settle out or be deposited. This process often leaves a line on the beach, known as a swash mark, to delineate the maximum excursion of that wave on the beach face (Figure 184). During a rising tide, the swash will progress farther and farther up the beach face, thus

Figure 184. Swash marks are left behind as the tide recedes and each wave leaves behind a line of beach debris. Photo Gary Griggs.

obliterating the swash marks of the earlier waves. But on a falling tide, successive waves gradually run a lesser distance up the beach face, such that a series of swash marks will be preserved.

Rill Marks: Sorting out the Sand

Waves washing back and forth on a sandy beach do not form cusps very often, but what they do more frequently is form rills or small channels, like miniature rivers (Figure 110). As the swash flows back down the beach face, it may erode little channels that can converge as tributaries to form larger channels. Because the beach face is not usually that steep or long, the rills are not normally very deep and do not extend for any great distance. In some cases, perhaps due to the change in slope or permeability of the beach sand, the rills may actually diverge or form distributaries proceeding down the beach face, much like the distributaries on a river delta.

Another type of rill mark forms where the backwash encounters an obstruction on the beach, perhaps a partially buried shell or pebble, and this causes the flow to diverge around the obstacle and leave small channels downslope (Figure 185). In many cases, with both types of rill marks, the shallow scour or erosion that takes place may expose slightly

Figure 185. Rill marks left in a geometric pattern by heavier and darker minerals. Photo Gary Griggs.

different colored sand, dark or heavy minerals, for example, that makes this rill mark more obvious.

Ripple Marks: A Corduroy Shoreline

As the tide goes out, many fine-grained sandy beaches display ripples or very small-scale troughs and ridges that have been formed by the flow of water over the sand surface. These patterns are often marked by concentrations of the darker or heavier minerals on the crests and lighter minerals like mica in the troughs.

The individual grains of sand on a beach are held in place by a combination of gravity and the friction between individual grains. In order for the grains to begin to move, either from the wind blowing over the dry beach or from water moving over the underwater portion of the beach, the wind or water has to be moving fast enough to overcome gravity and friction. The movement of water on the seafloor can be initiated by the passage of a wave, the backwash down the beach face, or can be driven by the flow of water out of a tidal inlet or draining of water that has accumulated on the backbeach. When the flow of water over a sandy surface reaches a certain velocity, it will begin to move individual sand grains. The larger or denser the grains, the faster the water has to be moving to dislodge them. At low velocities, individual sand

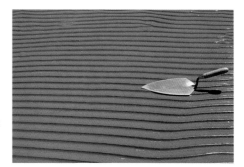

Figure 186. Very regular current ripples formed in mud in the Grand Canyon. Photo Dave Rubin, U. S. Geological Survey.

grains roll along the surface or bounce into each other, dislodging additional grains, which also start to move. As the velocity increases further, all the grains along the surface will begin to move, and soon small dunes or ripples begin to form.

Where the flow is dominantly in one direction, such as the water leaving an inlet or pond when the tide is going out, or along a riverbed, the ripples will be asymmetrical with a longer and gentler slope on the upstream, or upcurrent side, and a steeper slope on the downcurrent side (Figures 186 and 187). On the other hand, we can also observe oscillation ripples where the waves are moving the sediment back and forth on the seafloor and the ripples are symmetrical. Ripple marks

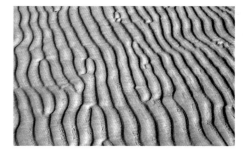

Figure 187. Current ripples formed in sand. Photo Dave Rubin U.S. Geological Survey.

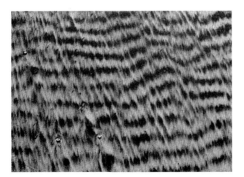

Figure 188. Intersecting current ripple and rill marks. Photo Gary Griggs.

usually form at right angles to the current direction and can be very uniform and parallel to one another, but they can also be more complex and crosscut one another where the water motion is more variable (Figure 188).

Beach Scarps: Watch Your Step

When you were a kid, do you recall walking or running along the low scarp or bank that had just been eroded into the beach and enjoying feeling the sand collapsing beneath your feet? These features are called beach scarps and form when the height or energy of the waves breaking along a particular beach has recently changed (Figure 189). As discussed in Chapter Six, beaches generally have either a winter/storm profile or a summer/swell profile. There are often times in spring or fall, however, when the wide summer berm is partially eroded by the arrival of steeper more energetic waves, which slice into the beach, eroding back the berm. This will leave a low scarp or cliff along the shoreline that may vary in height from a few inches to five feet or more, depending upon how high the berm has been built and how dramatic the change in wave energy has been. The larger and steeper waves are capable of cutting into the beach, eroding and suspending the sand, and transporting it back down the beach

Figure 189. A three-foot-high beach scarp left by storm waves. Photo Gary Griggs.

face. Almost overnight, a significant scarp can be created, although continuing wave action gradually smooths out the feature so it is much more subtle.

Patterns in the Rocks

While beaches can change hourly, producing many different features and landforms, such as those just described, rocks and the patterns they often express or contain are normally a product of thousands or millions of years. In some instances, the striking appearance of the rocks may just be the way those particular rocks formed initially, but, in other cases, the strange patterns may be a product of weathering or secondary processes that took place many eons later. Some are easier to understand and appreciate, whereas others inspire wonder. Then there are some odd things we cannot explain with certainty, so we can just appreciate them visually and not worry about why.

Contorted and Twisted: The Bedded Cherts of the Marin Headlands

When you drive across the Golden Gate Bridge, either entering or leaving San Francisco, you probably do not realize that within a few minutes of that world-famous and celebrated structure (Figure 190) are some fascinating rocks that contain an interesting and ancient bit of offshore history. If you turn towards the ocean onto Conzelman Road at the north end of the bridge, you will climb to some spectacular views of San Francisco and the bridge. But, if you look the other way, on the inland side of the road, you will pass a number of exposures of some highly contorted, evenly bedded dark brown rocks (Figure 191). These tightly folded and faulted rocks are radiolarian cherts and are all that remains of perhaps 100 million years of sea floor deposition of microscopic, planktonic animals that made their shells of silica. Radiolaria live in the upper ocean and form very delicate skeletons that

Figure 190. The Golden Gate Bridge and San Francisco as viewed from the Marin Headlands. Photo Gary Griggs.

Figure 191. Folded and contorted radiolarian cherts exposed in the Marin Headlands. Photo Gary Griggs.

settle to the sea floor when the animals die (Figure 192). They died by the trillions to form this roughly 250-foot thick layer of chert, which appears much thicker because of the way in which the rocks have been folded and contorted (Figure 30). We believe that the fossils accumulated in much lower latitudes and to the west, probably close to the equator, and were transported northeastward towards California over millions of years as plate motion progressed. Ultimately, the plates collided and these ancient seafloor sediments were plastered onto the edge of a much earlier California, perhaps 100 million years ago. Very similar rocks are found along the coastline south of the mouth of the Big Sur River. Being made of silica, with some iron that gives the brown, reddish-brown or maroon color, makes cherts extremely hard. They form very resistant and colorful pebbles that can be found on the nearby beaches.

Figure 192. Radiolaria are made of silica and have a wide range of shapes and patterns.

Black chert is found in the low cliffs and also on the beaches of Año Nuevo State Reserve in nearby San Mateo County. Here the chert is interbedded with 10 to 15-million-year-old siliceous shales and was probably originally derived from diatoms, the microscopic floating plants or pastures of the sea that also make siliceous skeletons (Figure 150). The black chert is nearly identical to obsidian, although has a completely different origin. The chert was discovered by the Native Americans who originally populated this coastline and was worked to make arrowheads and spear points. Because the chert is so hard, it will be gradually smoothed and polished as it is washed back and forth across the beach, or put into rock tumblers, which speed up the process of polishing and produce beautiful shiny pebbles (Figure 193).

Figure 193. Chert is a sedimentary rocks made of silica that was derived from diatoms or radioaria. Photo Gary Griggs.

Tafoni: Full of Holes

Sandstone bedrock outcrops along some of California's beaches often are pitted with small circular or elliptical holes known as tafoni, which leaves a honeycomb appearance (Figure 194). These irregularly-shaped depressions have smooth outlines and may be arranged in a somewhat regular or geometric pattern (Figure 195). They can vary widely in size from an inch or less to softball size or larger, although they tend to be somewhat uniform in size in any particular outcrop. The usually deep depressions are often so abundant that the pits constitute more of the rock outcrop than the sandstone itself. There is a general sense that the process of tafoni formation plays an important role in the retreat of the coastline.

While this weathering phenomenon is common along the California coastlines in coarse-grained sandstones, tafoni

Figure 194. An exsposure of tafoni at Pebble Beach along the San Mateo County coast. Photo Deepika Shresta Ross.

also occurs in desert or arid areas and has been recognized in volcanic, granitic, metamorphic, and other sedimentary rocks. Particularly striking examples of tafoni can be seen along the San Mateo coastline at Pebble Beach and also at Pt. Lobos State Reserve a few miles south of Carmel. In both places, they occur in coarse sandstones deposited by turbidity currents about 60 to 70 million years ago.

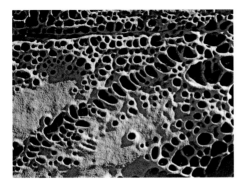

Figure 195. A close-up showing the intricate patterns of weathering in tafoni. Photo Deepika Shrestha Ross.

Much has been written about these widespread features. Like beach cusps, however, more is appreciated about their fascinating appearance than is understood or agreed upon regarding their origin. They do tend to form on vertical or steep outcrops, in contrast to horizontal surfaces. Currently favored explanations regarding their formation include salt weathering, wetting by seawater, and drying in the intertidal zone, as well as differential cementation, or variations in rock permeability. Tafoni seem to start as shallow pits, although why and when they start is not well understood. In some cases, the pits may form due to differences in the distribution of mineral grains or structural weaknesses within the rock that allow salt water, or the salt that crystallizes from the water, to etch, dissolve, or begin to break down small circular sections of rock. This process continues slowly over time as the pits deepen, expand, and eventually coalesce. Tafoni continues to be a curiosity wherever we find it and stimulates even non-scientists to ponder on its origin.

Concretions: Hard at the Center

You may have all seen concretions at one time or another, but wondered what they were or how they formed (Figure 196). Concretions can vary widely in size and shape but are generally spherical or ovoid and, typically, a few inches to a few feet across, and often have the appearance of large bowling or cannon balls. They are typically found in sedimentary rocks such as sandstones, siltstones, or mudstones, and are harder than the surrounding material, which causes them to weather out and remain as the softer encasing layers are removed. Concretions form in soft sediments prior to their hardening into rock when the pore spaces are filled with mineral cement, such as calcium carbonate, iron oxides, or silica. In some cases, the cementation within the pores of the sediment was initiated around some harder nucleus, such as a shell, bone, or tooth. Concretions appear different than the rocks that enclose them and often occur within certain layers

Figure 196. Weathering patterns in sedimentary rocks at Point Lobos showing exposed concretions. Photo Deepika Shrestha Ross.

or horizons or protruding from an outcrop or exposure. In some instances, they may actually be perched on pedestals (Figure 197). At times they have been mistaken for dinosaur eggs or some other fossil remains. They can be found in some sedimentary rocks making up the coastal cliffs and also exposed along the surfaces of marine terraces (Figure 198).

Figure 197. Concretions have weathered out of the sedimentary rocks exposed along the coastline of Taiwan. Photo Gary Griggs.

Figure 198. Concretions that have weathered out of the lowest marine terrace along the West Cliff Drive area of Santa Cruz. Photo Gary Griggs.

Bedrock Borings: Stuck in the Rock

Similar at first glance to tafoni, but on closer inspection quite different, are the circular holes found in the bedrock surface of the elevated marine terraces along the coastline (Figure 199). Where the terrace edge is exposed in the sea cliff along the present coastline, wave overtopping during high tides and winter storms will often erode or wash away the younger, looser, and more erodible overlying terrace deposits. This will leave the older bedrock surface bare and exposed (Figure 200). While overtopped by waves from time to time, this flat smooth surface is popular when dry with those who like to fish, sit and read, or just stand out as close as possible to the edge. But if you stop and look carefully at what is underfoot, you may find the bedrock has been extensively bored. A hundred thousand years ago, give or take a few thousand years, when this surface was being worn down in the surf zone, it was an area heavily populated by marine invertebrates. One of the common inhabitants along the California coast, then and today, are boring clams, known as

Figure 199. Pholad borings exposed on the surface of a marine terrace, although at this location the shells have been weathered away. Photo Gary Griggs.

pholads. These mollusks have deeply ribbed shells that enable them to drill or bore holes by rotating their shells. This same group of mollusks causes serious problems by boring into ship timbers and pilings, seriously weakening them.

As the clams grow larger, they continue to expand their homes in the intertidal zone by increasing the diameter and

Figure 200. Wave erosion has removed the unconsolidated sands on top of the lowest marine terrace. Notice the concretions (close-up in Figure 198) exposed on the terrace surface. Photo Gary Griggs.

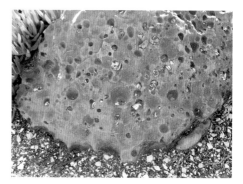

Figure 201. This sandstone concretion contains both pholad borings and also some of the shells that still remain in their growth positions. Photo Gary Griggs.

depth of their holes so they are deep enough to completely enclose their shells. This also protects them from any predators. Because the pholads are slightly pear-shaped, the bottom of the hole is larger than the entrance, which ends up trapping the clams in their self-made homes. They really cannot get out, but if you stop and think about it for a second, what would a clam do if it could escape from this bedrock prison? There are many locations where the shells of these 100,000 year old clams are exposed in their borings and can be seen either from the top of the terrace surface (Figure 201) or looking up from the beach below.

Sedimentary Intrusions: Quicksand Preserved

Molten lava driven upward by pressure from deep within the earth will intrude its way into the overlying rock, finding cracks and weaknesses to follow, and ultimately may emerge when it reaches Earth's surface to form lava flows, or even volcanoes. On its way to the surface, these volcanic intrusions gradually cool and harden. Where they followed horizontal routes, the lava will be preserved as sills, and where they followed vertical or near vertical pathways they are called dikes.

Intrusions of hot volcanic rock are common and pretty easy to understand. Somewhat surprisingly, there are also sedimentary or cold intrusions.

For 10 miles or so of the coastline of northern Santa Cruz County, sedimentary intrusions, or sandstone dikes and sills, have been well preserved in the sea cliffs. From the beaches of Wilder Ranch State Park to beyond the old cement town of Davenport, a bizarre variety of these unique features are exposed along the coastline. In some cases, they can actually be seen from State Hwy. 1 in roadcuts, without even getting out of your car; in other cases, a short walk to one of the pocket beaches will reveal some landforms not visible in many other places but well worth the trip (Figure 202).

While their origins are not completely clear, they were first recognized by an early field geologist who noticed them in the early 1900s in the cliffs north of Santa Cruz. The exposures of these intruded sandstones in the cliffs at Yellow Bank

Figure 202. Yellowbank Beach along the north coast of Santa Cruz County is named after the yellow- or orange- colored sandstone intrusions that make up nearly the entire sea cliff. This is the largest exposed sandstone intrusion known from anywhere in the world. Photo Kenneth and Gabrielle Adelman, California Coastal Records Project, www.CaliforniaCoastline.org.

Beach, several miles south of the small town of Davenport, are believed to be the largest exposures of this phenomenon above ground anywhere on Earth! The intrusive sandstones vary in color from yellowish or gold to gray and are distinctly different than the tan-colored, finer-grained mudstones they are found within. Some outcrops of the sandstone are oil-bearing and form natural asphalt, which was quarried at several sites a mile or two inland for years during the 1900s. This asphalt was reportedly transported to San Francisco in the early years of the last century to rebuild city streets following the San Francisco earthquake.

The sandstone intrusions are thought to have formed about seven to nine million years ago when petroleum and water saturated sands in the underlying geologic formation were liquefied and then injected upward into the overlying Santa Cruz Mudstone. The process of liquefaction is common during large earthquakes and can turn wet sediments into liquids, which allows them to flow. You can liquefy sand and create a localized area of quicksand by standing on the shoreline and moving your feet around in the wet sand. If fluid saturated sands are buried at depth, the overlying pressure may cause the sand to be forced upward, much like squeezing a tube of toothpaste (Figure 203). The exposures at Yellow Bank Creek are the largest and most extensive along the north coast of Santa Cruz County and are unique in the complexity of the bedding, the structures exposed in the rock and their coloration. It appears that there were several periods of intrusion with the grey, more resistant sandstone having been injected later than the gold colored sand (Figure 204). A major branch of the San Andreas Fault, the San Gregorio, lies just offshore in the Santa Cruz/Davenport area and movement along the fault has displaced a section of these intruded rocks to the Point Reyes area 70 miles to the north, where they also occur along the coastline. While these bizarre rock features have intrigued geologists for over a century, you can just appreciate them for their natural beauty and strange bedding patterns and not worry about how they formed.

Figure 203. Sea cliff exposure of two different generations of sandstone intrusions. The orange-colored sandstone was intruded first, followed by the gray vertical columns that were then injected upward into the orange sandstone. Photo Gary Griggs.

Spots in the Rocks

Some of the most interesting and fascinating features found in the rocks exposed along the coastline are products of more recent activity, long after the original rocks were formed.

Figure 204. Interbedded sedimentary intrusions from the same location as Figure 203 showing both orange and gray sequences. Photo Gary Griggs.

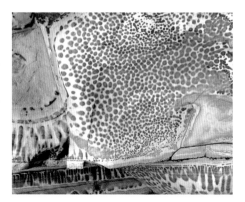

Figure 205. Spots formed by iron staining in mudstone at Natural Bridges State Beach in Santa Cruz. Photo Gary Griggs.

Exposure to ground water seepage, salt spray, runoff, and a variety of biological processes are capable of altering the appearance of the original rocks. The mudstone exposed in the cliff and rock platforms of Natural Bridges State Beach at the west end of the city of Santa Cruz are striking examples of these processes.

The surface of the tan-colored mudstone has been altered by a variety of distinct, brownish markings, some appearing like the spots on a leopard (Figure 205), while others are more concentric like tree rings (Figure 206). The brownish

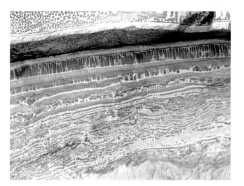

Figure 206. A complex pattern of iron staining within the Santa Cruz Mudstone. Photo Gary Griggs.

or rust color is almost certainly due to precipitation of iron oxide, and seems to be the result of ground water seeping into cracks and fractures within the mudstone. The fractures or joint patterns are usually due to the stress the rocks have been exposed to in the eons since they were formed, and these fractures tend to occur in geometric patterns. As the water seeps into the cracks, the iron contained in the water will gradually precipitate out, leaving rusty iron oxide marks behind as the water slowly dries out or evaporates. The stains will form in different geometric patterns based on the rock structure and weaknesses that the water has been able to penetrate. The leopard spotting results from the same iron oxide precipitation process but may be a result of microbial activity within the rocks that was spaced out somewhat uniformly within the cracks in the rocks and served as points where the iron could be precipitated more easily.

Trace Fossils: Ancient Footprints on the Seafloor

Everyone gets excited when they find a fossil and, often, the larger the fossil, the bigger the thrill. Whereas many of us may find shells exposed in the rocks of the cliffs during our coastal explorations, it is even more exciting to find whale-bones (Figure 207). Both of these are common in the two to five million year old sandstones and mudstones exposed in the cliffs between Capitola and New Brighton Beach along the shoreline of northern Monterey Bay (Figure 208). These fossils provide important evidence for geologists or paleontologists who are doing the detective work of trying to understand the origin of these particular sedimentary rocks.

Fifty miles south, in the sedimentary rocks of Point Lobos State Reserve, is some equally interesting evidence of early life, but from about 60 million years ago. In this case, however, rather than being actual fossils, or the preserved hard parts of some ancient organism, the rocks at Point Lobos

Figure 207. Fossil whale vertebrae and ribs from the sea cliff in Capitola. Photo Gary Griggs.

contain only traces of earlier life. The preserved footprints of early humans in East Africa or of dinosaurs in Wyoming are good examples of trace fossils. The patterns preserved in the rocks along the south shore of Point Lobos have captivated both photographers and geologists for decades. The sandstones and mudstones contain a wide range of burrows and trails left by different organisms (Figure 209), but the animals themselves were not preserved. So, while we do not know for certain exactly what the animals were, from the tracks we have a pretty good idea that they probably included worms, clams, as well as shrimp and crab-like animals.

Figure 208. Mollusk shells preserved in two- to five-million-year-old sandstone exposed in the coastal cliffs of northern Monterey Bay. Photo Gary Griggs.

Figure 209. Trails of approximately 60-million-year-old sea floor animals are preserved in the rocks of Point Lobos State Reserve south of Carmel. Photo Deepika Shrestha Ross.

The sediments that contain the trace fossils are dominantly turbidity-current deposits. We know from sea floor cores collected today that these underwater avalanches of mud and sand also have organic matter mixed in that has been transported into deeper water with the sediments. The density of the burrows and tracks preserved in the rocks indicate that there was plenty of food around to sustain these bottom dwelling organisms.

Some of the most interesting and striking features are the tracks of what was most likely some sort of crab, perhaps like a sand crab we might see scurrying along the beach face as the swash flows down the beach face. The trails preserve the imprints of what appear to have been feather like appendages on either side of the pathway or trail (Figure 210). While these trails are preserved on the flat surfaces of the sandstones and indicate that these animals lived and obtained their food from the seafloor itself, there are an entirely different set of burrows which pass vertically through the individual sediment layers. These were probably left by burrowing worms or, perhaps, shrimp-like crustaceans, that dug down into the mud to find their food. These burrows, some very small and some the size of your finger, are now usually filled with very light-colored sand so they stand out against the darker mud they burrowed into (Figure 211).

Figure 210. The tracks of a bottom-dwelling organism, perhaps something like a crab, exposed in the ancient rocks along the shoreline at Point Lobos. Photo Deepika Shrestha Ross.

Figure 211. An exposure of lighter turbidity-current deposits, or turbidites, interbedded with gray clays at Point Lobos. Looking carefully at the darker clays you can observe lighter colored sand-filled burrows extending down through the clay, where worms or other bottom dwellers worked their way through the sediment, ingesting the mud for its organic content. Photo Deepika Shrestha Ross.

These are all the sorts of features or remains that you could easily walk over simply because Point Lobos itself is such a remarkable scenic location with something to look at in every direction; the area that has been called "the most beautiful meeting place of land and sea on Earth." While there are many who have their own special place and might not completely agree, being able to walk along a 60-million year old seafloor and touch the tracks left behind by the primitive organisms that lived there at that time is an experience you should enjoy.

CHAPTER 9
LOOKING BACK
Some Final Thoughts

Having spent nearly my entire life either on the coast, or within an hour of it, has probably given me a little different perspective than many people. While some of my ancestors arrived on the East Coast on the Mayflower nearly 400 years ago, their descendants gradually worked their way across what was then the frontier, through New York, Ohio, Indiana, Illinois, Iowa, South Dakota, Nebraska and Kansas. Each generation pushed a little farther west. My mother's parents first reached the Pacific Coast in the Puget Sound area in the 1890s, which evidently appealed to them more than the wheat fields of Kansas and South Dakota, because they never went back. She and her family left Seattle for southern California in the 1920s when oil was discovered at Signal Hill near Long Beach.

My dad's father, who spent his earliest years in the flat lands of Iowa, bought a train ticket from St. Joseph, Missouri to San Francisco in 1901 for $25, and, at age 21, headed west. This was his first exposure to the Pacific coast, and while it would be a few years before he returned, he did come back and brought a young family to southern California in 1914. I have an old photograph of my father as a very young boy on a southern California beach taken about 1916, and another about 20 years later with a 90-pound, 12-foot-long, solid redwood surfboard, which he rode at San Onofre in the 1930s.

While I was born in Pasadena, I recall the occasional summer weekend trip to Long Beach or Huntington Beach to cool down. Years later, we moved to "The Valley." I have fond memories of heading off with friends to Zuma Beach, or to Malibu with my older brother, where I first surfed in 1959. Each summer as a kid, after my father finished teaching summer school, we packed up the family station wagon and headed north, out of the sweltering heat of the San Fernando Valley. We worked our way up the California coast, through the redwoods and on up the Oregon coast, camping in state parks for $1 a night. The 1950s were easy times for a kid, no wars that needed worrying about, no computers or Internet, no cell phones or iPods, just having fun and not wanting it to end and have to go back to school in September. Those summer trips and early adventures on the coast ingrained something in me that I later realized would need to be part of my adult life.

Heading to college at the University of California at Santa Barbara amplified these earlier experiences. Although I changed my major five times, I kept coming back to geology. When I was not in class learning about how Earth worked, I could surf or wander the beaches. It was all beginning to fit together and made more and more sense to me. Instead of cramming before midterms and finals, I usually walked on the beach or went surfing. Work and play began to merge. I discovered that there might be a way to sustain this path as a career, so on a whim decided to do graduate work in Ocean-ography. It was a good choice and ended up broadening my view beyond the solid earth to include waves, tides, currents, coastlines, and beaches, and an appreciation of how these all fit together.

I managed to finish a Ph.D. in three years, and in 1968, at 24, was offered an assistant professor position at the newly opened University of California at Santa Cruz. Although I had an offer to go to work for Exxon in Houston, Texas, exploring for offshore oil, academia and the coast of California won out. It was the right choice for me, and the next 42 years allowed me to focus much of my life and energy on the coast and beaches of California. Whether teaching about the ocean or studying the coastline and beaches, my interest in and appreciation of the coast of California continued to develop. Driving, biking, or hiking along the coastline and getting in the water when I can, have continued to be both play and work.

The westward migration for my ancestors came to a halt here on the shores of the Pacific Ocean. The ocean has been both an edge, and a border, and also a new frontier for many of us. There has always been something very reassuring and comforting to me about living on the coast, knowing there is wide-open ocean a few hundred feet away that stretches westward for thousands of uninterrupted miles.

So, since 1961, when I first began looking at beaches more carefully, I guess I have had a love affair with the California coast. Perhaps, like many of you, I've walked miles of beaches, taken thousands of pictures, collected hundreds of glass bottles full of different-colored sand, and have never grown tired of another day along the shoreline. I've seen the coast from the air and from the water. Two years ago, a friend and I led 35 people on a 30-mile-long, two-day beach walk completely around Monterey Bay. We combined history and geology and wore everyone out along the way. We all discovered that walking 30 miles on a sloping sand beach is not the same as 30 miles on a hiking trail. But you sure as heck see a lot of interesting things that you might otherwise never observe.

Over the past 42 years, I've observed a lot of changes along the coast. The population of California has doubled to 38 million and most of this growth has taken place in coastal counties. More people than ever, whether residents or visitors, come to the coast, and for lots of different reasons. It is a need or desire that many of us seem to have. Yet, we've had our impacts, fishing seasons closed, beaches posted, more seawalls, and a reduction in sand supplies to our beaches.

This book is my approach to try and explain how the coast and beaches of California have evolved, why they look like they do, and how they change over time. I think we can more fully appreciate this 1,100-mile-long coastline of ours if we better understand the forces and processes that operate along our western edge. Why does it look so different than Atlantic and Gulf coasts? How is our shoreline likely to change in the decades ahead?

There are also many unique and special places scattered along our coast, as well as lots of mysteries and features we do not completely understand. For me, these are some of the reasons why I come back day after day, and why I always look forward to another walk along the bluffs or another trip up or down the coast, looking for new places and new stories to unravel.

INDEX

Note: An f following a page number indicates a figure. Page numbers in **bold font** indicate major articles on the topic.

ABOUT THE AUTHOR

Gary Griggs is Director of the Institute of Marine Sciences and Professor of Earth and Planetary Sciences at the University of California, Santa Cruz. He is the co-author of *The Santa Cruz Coast: Then and Now* and *Living with the Changing California Coast* (UC Press), among other books. (Photo by Deepika Shrestha Ross.)

Series Design:	Barbara Haines
Design Enhancements:	Beth Hansen
Design Development:	Jane Tenenbaum
Composition:	Publication Services, Inc.
Text:	9.5/12 Minion
Display:	Franklin Gothic
Printer and binder:	Golden Cup Printing Company Limited

Introduction to California Mountain Wildflowers, Revised Edition, by Philip A. Munz, edited by Dianne Lake and Phyllis M. Faber

Introduction to California Spring Wildflowers of the Foothills, Valleys, and Coast, Revised Edition, by Philip A. Munz, edited by Dianne Lake and Phyllis M. Faber

Introduction to Shore Wildflowers of California, Oregon, and Washington, Revised Edition, by Philip A. Munz, edited by Dianne Lake and Phyllis Faber

Introduction to California Desert Wildflowers, Revised Edition, by Philip A. Munz, edited by Diane L. Renshaw and Phyllis M. Faber

Introduction to California Plant Life, Revised Edition, by Robert Ornduff, Phyllis M. Faber, and Todd Keeler-Wolf

Introduction to California Chaparral, by Ronald D. Quinn and Sterling C. Keeley, with line drawings by Marianne Wallace

Introduction to the Plant Life of Southern California: Coast to Foothills, by Philip W. Rundel and Robert Gustafson

Introduction to Horned Lizards of North America, by Wade C. Sherbrooke

Introduction to the California Condor, by Noel F. R. Snyder and Helen A. Snyder

Regional Guides

Natural History of the Point Reyes Peninsula, by Jules Evens

Sierra Nevada Natural History, Revised Edition, by Tracy I. Storer, Robert L. Usinger, and David Lukas

The **CALIFORNIA NATURAL HISTORY GUIDES** are the most authoritative resource on the state's flora and fauna. These short, inexpensive, and easy-to-use books help outdoor enthusiasts make the most of California's abundant natural resources. The series is divided into two groups: **INTRODUCTIONS** for beginners and **FIELD GUIDES** for more experienced naturalists. Please visit our web site for announcements, a regular natural history column, and the most up-to-date list of books. To hear about new guides through UC Press E-News, fill out and return this card, or sign up online at www.californianaturalhistory.com.*

Name _____

Address _____

City/State/Zip _____

Email _____

Which book did this card come from? _____

_____

Where did you buy this book? _____

_____

What is your profession? _____

Comments _____

WE'D LOVE TO HEAR FROM YOU!

* UC Press will not share your information with any other organization.

Return to:

University of California Press

Attn: Natural History Editor

2120 Berkeley Way

Berkeley, California 94704-1012